Ryan *and* Ronnie

HYWEL GWYNFRYN

Gomer

To Anja, my wife,
for her love and constant support

Published in 2014 by
Gomer Press, Llandysul, Ceredigion, SA44 4JL

ISBN 978 1 84851 847 6

A CIP record for this title is available from the British Library.
© Text: Hywel Gwynfryn 2014

Photographs: © BBC Cymru Wales by kind permission

Hywel Gwynfryn asserts his moral right under
the Copyright, Designs and Patents Act 1988,
to be identified as the author of this work.

Printed and bound in Wales at
Gomer Press, Llandysul, Ceredigion
www.gomer.co.uk

Contents

Foreword

The middle of the twentieth century is a strange time for the Welsh. The 1960s in particular see Wales at odds with the rest of the world. America is caught in the upheaval of the civil rights movement, free love and anti-Vietnam protests. Europe has serious student unrest, Britain is plagued with strikes and Ireland is in flames.

On the surface, nothing much seems to change here, though. In many ways, the old clichés still apply – the heavy industries of steel and coal are still the core of our economy, rugby is still king, and working men's clubs and institutes are thriving.

As we all know, the dragon has two tongues – Welsh and English – and tensions between the two are about to reach fever pitch. The Welsh language, for so long derided by some as the language of the second rate and unambitious, is finding its voice and expressing itself as a powerful political force. It is also finding its feet in broadcasting.

Suddenly, *Cymru* and *Cymraeg* are becoming cool. Although the cultural icons of the old guard – the Eisteddfod in particular – still have clout, a younger, less deferential element is gaining ground, demanding change, something new – a bit of fun!

Against this backdrop, two very different characters would be thrown together. Ryan Davies, the ultimate all-rounder, showman, comic, song and dance man, and Ronnie Williams, no stranger to the stage himself, but not so 'flash', an actor and a writer more than anything else.

It was obvious that these two had something different. They had a new approach to entertainment. They each drove a white Jaguar. Their suits were superbly cut, they wore stage make-up, had a proper PA and lighting system, and a fully qualified stage manager to operate it all. They filled the halls and theatres of Wales with huge audiences. People were amazed.

I was amazed.

This Welsh Wales was completely unknown to me, a monoglot Cardiff kid with his head full of the folk songs of Ireland and Scotland, not to mention the gems of Woody Guthrie, early Bob Dylan and Tom Paxton floating across the Atlantic.

My group, the Hennessys, had been living in Ireland between 1968 and 1969, and on our return to Cardiff we were invited to audition for a Welsh-language TV show called *Disc a Dawn*, and a network English-language series called *Singing Barn*. Luckily for us, Merêd, who had brought Ryan and Ronnie together, decided we'd do, and we set about learning songs in Welsh, which is when I first came across Hywel Gwynfryn.

Hywel worked for BBC TV and radio. He had a real gift for adapting and translating songs into Welsh. He became a good friend of the group – he still is – and pretty soon, we were all involved touring with Ryan and Ronnie – and what a time we had. At the end of one tour, I owed the company £28.00. Not much to show for a fortnight's work.

What Hywel manages to do so successfully here is to capture the mood of the nation at a particular time in our history, and give us a real insight into two talented, troubled individuals, who combined to create something very special indeed: sparkling entertainment. Sadly, both Ryan and Ronnie, for very different reasons, would be dead before their time. But for a few precious years, they would drive Welsh TV and theatre to new heights.

I know that Hywel and I will never forget them.

Neither, I suspect, will many of you.

Frank Hennessy

Llandaff, August 2014

To begin at the end ...

A quarter to midnight on the twenty-first of December 1997. Two policemen are questioning the owner of a car on Cardigan bridge. A wild-looking man walks towards them from the direction of Morgan Street. Unsteady on his feet, he leans heavily on his stick. Ten minutes later, the car drives away and the policemen walk off. The man is still there, staring after them, waiting for them to disappear.

He turns and walks slowly in the direction of the river. He has been to this place several times before, but he's changed his mind every time. Tonight, there will be no turning back. The final decision has been made. He places his stick carefully against the wall of the bridge and stares at the river, judging the distance he has to fall. Torrential rain has caused the level of the water to rise. The swollen river below waits eagerly to embrace him.

Over the Christmas period, families all over Cardigan, and in villages and towns throughout Wales, will laugh at Ryan Davies cavorting on their television screens dressed as a Christmas fairy, and Ronnie Williams playing Dai Bach y Blagard in the situation comedy *Licyris Olsorts*. After all, it wouldn't be Christmas without Ryan and Ronnie.

In the midst of their Christmas festivities, the sipping of Babycham and the munching of chocolates, the happy families are blissfully unaware that Ronnie's body is floating in the river Teifi. The river has kept her secret, and carried his body gently for seven days before depositing it on the rocks at St Dogmaels, the final resting place on his painful journey, which began fifty-eight years earlier in Cefneithin.

Ryan's early years

Cabaret night in a club, somewhere in Wales. Ryan walks on stage to the sound of the Bennie Litchfield band playing the introduction to 'New York, New York'. The spotlight hits him. He grabs the mike. 'Start spreadin' the news, I'm leavin' today, I want to be a part of it, New York, New York.' Three minutes later he's in full swing, walking towards the band, crossing the stage to the audience, picking out individual faces and singing to them personally: 'If I can make it there, I'll make it anywhere ...' He signals the band to stop. It's the big finish. 'It's up to you New York! New York!' The final notes of the Frank Sinatra classic are drowned out by the applause of a very appreciative audience. Ryan bows repeatedly and then addresses the expectant audience in a Swansea accent:

'Evening ladies and gentlemen ... Nice to see you.' (He scans the beaming audience.) 'I must say, the ladies have made an effort tonight. Good God, girls, you look like a garden of flowers ... No, honestly, you do ... a beautiful garden.' (The girls laugh. Ryan pauses.) 'Mind you, it could do with a bit of weeding here and there.' (Laughter.) 'I come from Glanaman. My grandmother had a ranch on the side of the Black Mountain.' (The audience laughs. Ryan pauses.) 'To be honest, it was more of a farm really, well, not so much a farm as a smallholding.' (More laughter as the original 'ranch' diminishes rapidly in size.) 'Alright! I won't lie. It was a cottage ... (laughter) with two cows and a sow.' (More laughter.)

No-one worked an audience like Ryan. He knew instinctively that two cows and a sow were far funnier than two sheep and a hen, or two pigs and a bull. After all, he came from a very talented family – the Roberts of the Mountain. Mountain View was the house where his grandmother and his mother Nans were born. His grandfather John Roberts, known as John Roberts the Reciter, had won the main recitation prize in the Swansea National Eisteddfod in 1907, the year the English Rugby Union bought a little piece of land called Twickenham. And he scored again at the Carmarthen Eisteddfod in 1911.

Thomas Ryan Davies was born on 22 January 1937. Thomas was his father William Davies' middle name, a collier whose hobby was fishing. After a whole week underground working the coal in cramped, dark, airless conditions, he liked nothing better than walking along the banks of the Cothi and Tywi rivers, trying to persuade the fish to take the bait with a swish of his rod. Many years later, in an interview with Pat Searle, the fishing columnist of the *Western Mail*, Ryan was at pains to stress that his father was a strong believer in the sanctity of life, and therefore treated the fish like pieces of fine Dresden china, returning them to the river after they'd been caught. William Davies left his fishing tackle to his son in his will, but Ryan didn't share his father's enthusiasm for the sport, preferring to do most of his fishing during sketches in his television shows.

> *Ryan is seen sitting on a stool, dressed as a fisherman. He is, however, sitting in the middle of a field. A young girl walks by, and stops.*
>
> Girl: Are you fishing?
> Ryan: Yes!
> Girl: (*looking bewildered*): But I can't see any water anywhere. How many have you caught?
> Ryan: You're the fourth!

Although Ryan's father liked fishing, his great love was music. He conducted a local choir and played the organ in Nant Chapel, both from the copy and improvised, when the fancy took him, a rare gift he passed on to his son, who had a keen ear for music. Ryan's musical prowess even became a part of one of his and Ronnie's routines:

Ryan: Hey, Ron.

Ronnie: Yes, Ry.

Ryan: Did you know that I could play the piano by ear?

Ronnie: Can you really? By ear?

Ryan: No, Ron. Not by there. By 'ere!

Ronnie: *(grabs Ryan by his shirt front. They are now staring at each other, noses touching)* RYAN!

Ryan: No, seriously Ron. I *can* play by ear.

Ronnie: *(releases Ryan from his grip, reluctantly)* Really. Is it difficult?

Ryan: No, Ron. It's not difficult, but I get a hell of a headache when my ear hits the keyboard.

Sometimes, after a late concert in the local hall, Ryan and Ronnie would go to the pub. The doors would be locked, drinks bought and Ryan would sit at the piano playing a variety of songs in various styles. 'Sosban Fach', for instance, would be given a dramatic Tchaikovsky-style opening, and the verses that followed would be played in the style of Mozart, Bach, Beethoven and even Russ Conway. There is a story told about the very young Ryan telling his father, who had just returned from the war, that he'd been having music lessons, and, like a true performer, he was obviously keen to show his father how good he was. William was indeed agreeably surprised at his son's technique, since he was not only playing from the copy, but adding improvised phrases at will. Like father, like son. Ryan surpassed even the great Les Dawson in the extremely difficult art of playing the piano with feeling and emotion, whilst playing completely out of tune at the same time, on purpose of course, making anyone within earshot double up with laughter.

Another talented member of the family was Ryan's aunt Peggy – Peggy Wheelhouse, another winner at the National Eisteddfod – who kept the village shop on the square in Betws, the village where Jim Griffiths, Wales' first Secretary of State, was born. According to T. J. Davies, Peggy sold everything to everyone:

> Hidden underneath the dolls' eyes, coffin nails, liquorice allsorts and bootlaces was a pile of books in Welsh. She had a Welsh soul. She loved books, she loved poetry and she loved to recite and compete.

If Peggy had competed at the Bala Eisteddfod in 1967, she would have seen her nephew take to the stage for the first time as the comic half of the most famous double act Wales had ever seen – Ryan and Ronnie.

The roll call of Ryan's talented family members is very impressive. His Uncle Ivor was an opera producer and an impresario. A prominent member of the Aman Valley Operatic Society, he usually sang the main role. In those early days, the whole area was a hive of musical and cultural activity. Children of Ryan's age were given an opportunity to sing, dance, act, write, and play musical instruments. There were operatic societies in Garnant, Gwauncaegurwen, Ammanford and Cwmllynfell, performing to capacity audiences every night, and Uncle Ivor was responsible for producing a number of those operas over the years.

If you happened to be a member of the audience in Ammanford Hall on a Thursday night for the local eisteddfod, you could expect to be there until the early hours of Sunday morning, listening to six chapels competing against each other.

Uncle Ivor always made sure that he had complimentary tickets for members of the family to see his lavish productions. But on one occasion, no tickets were available for his production of *King's Rhapsody*, since he needed every penny from ticket sales to cover costs, which amounted to a thousand pounds, according to Uncle Ivor. He explained his predicament to the family in Welsh, but in order to drive home how expensive this production was, he would insist on repeating the price many times in English, whilst waving the tickets in the air. 'One thousand pounds … Chi'n deall? ONE THOUSAND POUNDS!'

The star of the family before Ryan came along was another uncle, Morgan Rhys Roberts. Uncle Morgan's forte was acting, and indeed the BBC recognised his thespian prowess by putting him on contract. According to Ryan himself: 'My mother's brother, Uncle Morgan, was quite a character, and we're very alike. Without a doubt, he had a great influence on me.' In 1965, thiry years after Uncle Morgan's success, Ryan was also given a full-time television contract by the BBC's Light Entertainment Department, the first of its kind in the history of broadcasting in Wales.

Paying tribute to Ryan after his death in 1977, Jennie Eirian, then editor of the Welsh-language newspaper *Y Faner*, mentioned the importance of the family's influence on the young Ryan Davies: 'Ryan was a link in a very valuable chain, and it's important that every link is strong and durable. Because the strength of the family chain strengthens the life of the nation.'

The radio and television producer Ivor Rees, who gave Ryan his first opportunity on the radio, went a step further and emphasised

Ryan's ability to bring Welsh – and English – language cultures together:

> Without a doubt, Ryan Davies was the best entertainer seen in Wales in the twentieth century, and it's important to remember that his bilingual upbringing combined two cultures. On the one hand, he was immersed in the Welsh-language culture of the chapel and the eisteddfod, and on the other, he embraced the sophisticated world of the television and stage entertainer. He was just as happy in the chapel vestry as he was later on in life with audiences in cabaret, clubs and theatres all over Wales.

Years later, Ryan echoed those words in one sentence, which is engraved on a bust of his head in the foyer of the BBC in Llandaff: 'Laughter is the same in both languages.'

Ryan was quite used to the sound of an audience laughing and applauding from a very early age. A hundred yards from his home in Mountain View, at the top of Tircoed Street in Glanaman, was a pub called the Angel. While his mother and his Auntie Anne were in a prayer meeting, Ryan, so the story goes, would walk into the Angel, bold as brass, stand on one of the tables and sing to the men at the bar, who would give him a few pennies for entertaining them. He soon progressed from the tabletop performance to the mid-week meeting in Sunday school, eventually reaching the dizzy heights of the pulpit in Capel Mawr, Bryn Seion, Glanaman. Nans was more than happy to admit that she was Ryan's mother. 'When you remember,' she'd say, 'that the whole family loved performing, it's no wonder that he became a performer too. It was in his blood.' Nans was Ryan's biggest fan, and she herself was a member of a local choir. Having left school at the age of fourteen, she went on to entertain the residents of the workhouse in Ffair-fach before finding permanent work in the sewing room there. She was very proficient at making shirts and flannel underwear for the men and woollen frocks for the girls to keep them warm during the winter months, and light cotton blouses with a white stripe for summer wear. Years later, Nans looked after a childrens' home in Nantgaredig, a small village to the east of Carmarthen on the banks of the Tywi river. By that time, she and 'Wili Tom' were married, and they became the matron and master of several homes in Llangadog, Llandovery, Felin-foel, and finally, a home called Y Dolydd, in Llanfyllin, fourteen miles south-west of Oswestry in Montgomeryshire. Y Dolydd was known locally as the Union Workhouse, and looked more like a prison than the home Ryan had lived in for the first ten years of his life. It was a cold, stone-grey, unwelcoming Victorian building, reminiscent of those bleak houses decribed by Charles Dickens in his novels. Indeed, you almost expected Magwitch or Fagin to walk by and inquire 'What's your name, boy?', especially since Y Dolydd was a welcoming refuge for any rough-looking tramp, who would be expected to pay for his overnight stay by breaking stones in the yard before leaving in the morning. Iago the musician, Mr Redhead, Mr Hughes-who-never-wore-a-shirt and their friends all knew that Nans and Wili Tom would never turn them away.

Ryan's school friend at this time was David Williams, who lived above the workhouse in Brynffynnon. He also remembers the colourful characters who stayed at Y Dolydd, especially one-eyed Bobbie Burns who, in spite of his disability, could carve and fashion ships out of wood, which he decorated with silver paper. David and Ryan became close friends, and one of the games they enjoyed playing involved frightening their friends out of their wits. The graveyard next to the workhouse was an ideal hiding place for two young boys dressed in white bedsheets, waiting to jump out in front of unsuspecting children on their way to school on a dark morning. On a rainy Saturday, they'd play indoors with Ryan's Hornby trains layout until the sun came out, which meant they could go and catch rabbits, collect birds' eggs or do some fishing. Their way of fishing was far removed from Ryan's father's careful, humane approach and was very dangerous as well. It involved placing a lump of carbide with a hole in it inside an empty syrup tin. The tin would then be dropped into a pool in the river, and the boys would wait for the ensuing explosion. A primitive way of catching fish, perhaps, but nevertheless fairly effective, judging by the number of very dead fish that would float, wide-eyed, to the surface of the pool.

Eiry Palfrey, who was eight years of age at the time and also lived in Llanfyllin, remembers Ryan as 'a confident schoolboy, fluent in both languages.' Confidence, style, and natural all-round talent – Ryan had all the necessary attributes to be what he became, one of the most talented professional bilingual entertainers Wales has ever seen. Even at this early age, he was an accomplished performer, and he could whistle and imitate birdsong as well as dance, sing, act and play the harp. Of course, the residents of the workhouse provided him with a ready-made audience too. When he moved to the local secondary school, there were plenty of opportunites to act in school plays in Welsh and English, and he was also a member of the local amateur dramatics company, the Myllin Players. When a new wing was added to the school, Ryan's tenor voice was heard in the opening ceremony, where he took the leading role in a performance of Haydn's *The Seasons*, sharing the limelight with another star of Llanfyllin Secondary School, who became a world-famous opera star – Elizabeth Vaughan. Ryan was also an accomplished sportsman. He played in goal for his school and for the local Llanfyllin football team.

Montgomeryshire School cricket team could testify to his prowess with the bat, and he showed Gerald Davies-like speed on the wing when he played rugby, even though he suffered from asthma – a condition he inherited from his mother. After one particularly virulent attack, it was decided to send him back to Glanaman to recuperate because his parents were so busy looking after the residents in the home. And indeed, when he arrived, he received a warm bardic welcome from his uncle, Brinley Richards, who later became Archdruid of the Eisteddfod. Brinley wrote seven couplets, which were in fact instructions for Ryan as to how he was expected to behave and what he should do if he wanted to get better. He had to eat often, and drink a glass of milk with an egg in it daily. He had to go to bed early and, most importantly, he wasn't to bother his grandmother. In addition to the milk and egg concoction, Ryan was also given Robelene, a medicine for tight chests or asthma. It worked for a while, but it wasn't a miracle cure, and Ryan had to live with the condition and its effects all his life, until he eventually died of a fatal asthma attack in America at only forty years of age.

Feeling much stronger after his stay at Mountain View, he returned to school in Llanfyllin and was immediately selected for the school's dance party, which competed that year at the International Eisteddfod in Llangollen. At the age of fifteen he added another string to his bow, as he revealed in an interview later in life:

> When I was fifteen, I was given a small harp as a present from my auntie, and was fortunate enough to have lessons from Nancy Richards, Wales' foremost expert on the triple harp. I used to go to the farm at Pen-y-bont Fawr after school to have tea with her, and then she'd

give me a lesson. The lesson didn't last very long, and it quickly turned into a concert, with Nancy singing to her own harp accompaniment while I just sat by the fire and watched. My father would call for me at eight, and then we'd both stay until midnight. And that's how it was every time. I remember competing at one eisteddfod, singing and playing the harp, as well as in several other categories. In fact, I was on the stage so often that the compere turned to the audience and said: 'This young boy Bryan is on the stage more often than I am!'

One of the many eisteddfodau he attended, and one of the most important ones as far as Ryan was concerned, was the one held at Llanrhaedr-ym-Mochnant in mid-Wales in 1947. It was here that he met Irene, the daughter of Harri and Mary Williams, and the girl who was to become his wife. 'I think he fancied me a bit,' was Irene's comment after talking to him. But four years went by before they became proper sweethearts. Irene remembers Ryan as a young boy who loved games, and performing, 'but didn't pull out all the stops academically'. He hated exams, partly because he worried about them, and the extra pressure always brought on a bout of asthma. Of course, if he'd spent more time studying and less time performing, he might have gone to university and we might never have heard of him. In 1957, however, Ryan went to the Normal College in Bangor, a move which changed his life completely. He said of that time: 'It was at the Normal College that I matured as a person, and met people who shared my love of drama and performing.'

But before he could attend the Normal, he first had to perform his national service. On 13 September 1954, at eighteen years of age, Ryan joined the Royal Air Force.

Ronnie's early years

The views from Llyn Llech Owain on a sunny summer's day are breathtaking. They stretch south towards the Gwendraeth valley, east towards the Amman valley and north in the direction of Carreg Cennen Castle. And when Lyn, Ronnie's widow, scattered his ashes on the surface of the lake after his funeral, that simple gesture completed his tortuous journey back to his roots. Ronnie and the boys of Cefneithin village used to swim in the lake summer and winter, despite repeated warnings from teachers and parents that the submerged roots of water lilies below the surface could wrap themselves around your legs and drag you down to the bottom of the dark lake, where fish with large teeth were ready to ravage your body, rip you to shreds, and swallow you whole. If such an attack had been launched against Ronnie by any dark forces in the lake, he might have escaped, being a strong swimmer. In fact, he preferred swimming to rugby and soccer, according to one of his school friends:

> Ron hated going to the gym, playing rugby and kicking a soccer ball. He always had a headache, or an appendicitis pain or an ingrowing toenail – any old excuse. At the end of one term, his teacher wrote on his report: 'I am surprised that Ronnie, medically, survived the term.'

His friends played cricket on the field across the way from Ronnie's house in Cefneithin, but there was never any guarantee that Ronnie would join them. Indeed, as a young boy, he was happy in his own company and would often walk by the lake rehearsing lines from *Macbeth* or *Julius Caesar* for the annual school play. Even at an early age, Ronnie wanted to be an actor, and in later interviews he often referred to 'Dai Sais' – Ralph Davies from Pontycymmer, his inspirational English teacher – who opened his eyes to the greatness of Shakespeare's plays and Dylan Thomas' poetry. Sometimes, late in the evening, Ronnie's young soprano voice could be heard singing Eli Jenkins' prayer from *Under Milk Wood* from the direction of the lake.

> We are not wholly bad or good
> Who live our lives under Milk Wood
> And Thou, I know, wilt be the first
> To see our best side, not our worst.

Ronnie's best friend was Nigel Rees, who remembers going to Ronnie's house to sing pop songs by the Everly Brothers around the piano, with Ronnie playing the accompaniment to 'Cathy's Clown' and 'Dream'. He was also keen to show his acting talents, and his was the first hand in the air when Tommy Scourfield or the legendary Carwyn James, who ran the local youth club, were looking for volunteers to act in the next production on the stage of the Miners' Welfare Hall in Ammanford. One year, he acted in a play about the source of a historical local site. The story goes that Owain, one of King Arthur's knights, visited the area on horseback. Feeling thirsty, he dismounted by a well, removed the slate slab cover, drank his fill and fell asleep, forgetting to replace the slate (*llech* in Welsh). As a result, the well overflowed, flooding the surrounding countryside and forming a lake named after the slate and the knight – Llech Owain. Ronnie played the starring role of the sleepy, careless knight. Buddug Williams, who plays the role of Anti Marian in the soap opera *Pobol y Cwm*, remembers acting with Ronnie in the local youth club. Indeed, the desire to perform anything, anywhere and at any time, was as strong in Ronnie as it was in Ryan. He could write very funny sketches as well, like the one about Jemima, a lady of dubious reputation, who was very blessed in the upper regions. Ronnie not only wrote the sketch, but also played the part of big-breasted Jemima, and his friend Eryl played Jemima's husband, who has been called up to join the army leaving flirty Jemima free to 'entertain' the mikman, the postman, the butcher and anyone else who ventured to knock on her door. Unfortunately, Eryl couldn't remember a single line of the script, but he could remember the enormous pantomime breasts that Ronnie was wearing. There was no doubt in Eryl's mind that the success of the Jemima sketch, and the fun they had acting it, was the main reason why Ronnie became a performer. Another sketch written and performed by Ronnie whilst still at Gwendraeth Grammar School, which in later years became one of the most popular sketches of Ryan and Ronnie's television series, was 'Tŷ Ni' ('Our House'). Mam was played by Ryan and Wil, the father, by Ronnie. Their son and daughter, Nigel Wyn – named after Ronnie's school friend Nigel Rees – and Phyllis Doris, were played by Derek Boote (and later by Bryn Willams) and Myfanwy Talog. Nigel Wyn was as thick as the proverbial two short planks, and Phyllis Doris was common as muck. Every week without fail, as she sawed her way through another loaf of bread tucked under her arm, Mam would lose her temper with Phyllis Doris, and Wil would shout the line that became the catchphrase of the series at Nigel Wyn: 'And don't call Wil on your father!'

Ronnie was in his element writing, acting, producing, directing and presenting various school productions at Gwendraeth and in other schools in the area. According to Eryl, he and Ronnie had already planned their future:

We were starstruck. Fame and fortune were waiting for us in Stratford and on the West End stage. For years we dreamt of being successful actors someday, doing what we loved doing best of all *and* getting paid for it.

When you compare Ronnie's and Ryan's upbringings, the similarities are obvious. Both were products of a coal-mining community with solid cultural foundations. Singing, acting and competing in local eisteddfodau, as well as performing in the village hall, were an important part of everyday life. They were both born performers, and the opportunities they were given to appear in front of an audience when they were young gave them the confidence they would need later on in life in television studios, in cabaret clubs and on theatre stages in both Wales and England. And, of course, there were strong family influences – Ryan's grandfather, uncle, aunt and mother on the one hand, and in Ronnie's case, his own father Iori, who was one half of the popular comedy duo Sioni and Iori.

Iori worked at the Blaenhirwaun pit until the 1950s, when he had an accident at work and had to give up his job as a miner. He was small and round like his wife May, always wore a smile and liked his whisky. May had a no-nonsense way about her, according to Margaret her niece, and she was quite happy to give you her opinion even if you hadn't asked for it. Years later, May and Iori kept a number of pubs in Carmarthenshire, including the Black Horse in Carmarthen, which was renamed y Ceffyl Du by Ronnie in the 1960s, according to actress Sharon Morgan. She remembers some very late evenings in the Ceffyl Du, when the pub and the glasses would be full to overflowing, and Iori would climb on the table, whisky glass in hand, to sing and tell jokes like he did in the old coal-mining days with Sioni, his partner.

In her book about the Gwendraeth valley, Nan Evans draws a vivid picture of the miners walking to the pit on the early morning shift:

> We never saw them going to work. It was still dark. But we could hear the noise of their hobnailed boots on the stone streets. We saw the afternoon shift coming home. Strange men with blackened faces, coughing their way up the hill. Some walked together in clusters, others by themselves, stopping now and then for another drag on the cigarette, or just to gasp for breath. Every miner carried his snap-box and a flask of tea in his pocket, and a block of wood under his arm to light the fire. These were the coal-miners. These were our fathers.

And these were the men that Ronnie remembered in a poem he wrote in Welsh when he revisited Cefneithin many years later to make a programme about the village where he was born.

> The hill is steep, and threaded with a black ribbon along its length.
> Colliers coughing and spitting, leaving their mark
> And we, with our satchels on our backs, barely notice them.
> 'Keep at it,' they shout,
> Glad that we'd been given a chance that they had not.

And there were plenty of opportunities for anyone who felt the inclination to sing or act to develop that talent. Children were nurtured in the Sunday service, the local concerts and the *Cymanfa Ganu* held on Easter Monday in Tabernacl chapel, or in Bethania in Tumble, which was within easy walking distance across the railway line from Cefneithin. After the afternoon meeting, tea was served in the vestry, with *bara brith* (Welsh tea bread) or currant cake and bread and cheese as well. In the evening, the chapel would resound to the oratorios of J. Ambrose Lloyd, Christmas Williams and 'The Heavens Declare the Creator's Glory' by Haydn. Every little village in the Gwendraeth valley held its own eisteddfod, where the stars of the day, like Lyn Richards, Gwyneth Beynon and Anita and Pegi Williams sang their hearts out to the visiting adjudicators. The Mecca for anyone who enjoyed the opera or a good play was the Hall in Cross Hands. The Mynydd Mawr Operatic Society performed *Hansel and Gretel*, *The Bartered Bride* and *Cavalleria Rusticana* there. Three famous drama companies also brought the house down when they acted on the hall's famous stage: Dan Mathews' company from Pontarddulais, Ivor Thomas' from Pont-henri and Edna Bonnell's company from Llanelli. This is how one local historian describes the Cross Hands Hall at the time:

> The stage was as wide as the sea, and the hall was very sumptuous. There were plush seats and velvet curtains, and immediately in front of the stage was the orchestra, waiting for Tommy Lewis to raise his baton. Under the stage, the changing rooms were a hive of activity, people shouting 'Hisht!' and some shaking like leaves whilst waiting to go on and perform. One or two, who were braver than the rest, slipped upstairs to peep through the curtains, and then returned shouting excitedly, 'It's packed out!'

It always was a packed house for the performance of any play by Gwyn D. Evans, the local playwright, who became one of the scriptwriters of *Pobol y Cwm* in its early days. But his name was also associated with a concert party full of local talent, which he established in 1947. The stars of the party were Sioni and Iori, with their entertaining mix of a smile and a song, a successful recipe which was adopted and adapted by Ronnie and Ryan twenty years later. Another party from the area, the Trwpadŵrs, became one of the most famous concert parties in Wales. In fact, according to the posters, apart from being 'BBC artists', they were also 'Wales' Premier Singing Group', having performed with Norman Vaughan, David Lloyd and the Dallas Boys. Ronnie himself shared the stage with the Trwpadŵrs in a one-act play produced by the school. One of their greatest fans was the singing legend Dorothy Squires, who was born in Pontyberem, a few miles down the road from Cefneithin. She invited the concert party to join her on a tour of Australia. According to Lyn Roberts, one of the Trwpadŵrs:

> Everbody shouted 'All right!'. We all wanted to go to Australia with Dorothy, but when we got home and told our wives, common sense prevailed. Well, we had to earn a living, so that was the end of that.

This was the cultural tradition that Ronnie was steeped in, and there were plenty of opportunities for him to shine. But, as was mentioned earlier, the greatest influence on Ronnie was his father. In an interview he gave two years before his death in 1997, he reminisced about his childhood. When VE Day was announced, Cefneithin – like hundreds of other villages and towns throughout Wales – held street parties to celebrate the end of the war. He could remember being lifted up on to a long trestle table covered in a white tablecloth and plates full of sandwiches. The celebrations were held on 8 May 1945. Ronnie was just six years old. 'I was very plump and very, very small. Like a shorter version of my father, who had written verses for me to sing at the village party while his mate Sioni played the piano.'

When he was twelve, Ronnie joined his father and Sioni on the road and on stage. Before he left the house, his mother made sure that her son was smartly dressed, with a parting in his thick black hair. According to Nigel, his school friend, 'he looked like a tailor's dummy'. While his mother dressed him up, his father gave him advice as to how he should stand on stage and communicate with his audience. In a nutshell, his advice was: 'Watch me, and you'll learn something.' So Ronnie stood out of sight in the wings, watched and learned how to introduce a song, how to tell a joke and, above all, the importance of timing, especially during quick-fire patter. This became invaluable years later, as in this sketch:

Ronnie: That's a nice watch you're wearing, Ry.

Ryan: You like it, Ron?

Ronnie: I do, Ryan. It looks expensive.

Ryan: You are not mistaken in the assumption you have made, Ron. It was. Very expensive.

Ronnie: Is it a special watch, Ry?

Ryan: Ron. Let me tell you how special this watch. (*Ronnie waits for the explanation. Ryan is smiling at the studio audience and showing the watch to them. Ronnie is slowly losing his temper, and speaks sharply to Ryan.*)

Ronnie: Go on then.

Ryan: Go where, Ron?

Ronnie: I mean tell us about the watch.

Ryan: Ah! Yes! This watch. Well, Ron. It's dust-proof.

Ronnie: Yes.

Ryan: Shockproof.

Ronnie: Yes.

Ryan: Waterproof. And ... (*Ryan pauses. Ronnie waits. Ryan looks at Ronnie.*) I'm not happy with it.

Ronnie: (*looks shocked and exasperated*) What? You're not happy with an expensive-looking watch that's dust-proof, waterproof, and shockproof. WHY?

Ryan: (*looks down at the watch and up at Ronnie before delivering the punchline.*) Bloody thing caught fire last week!

Back with Sioni and Iori, and on queue, Ronnie would appear on stage to keep the audience entertained while Sioni and Iori slipped out for a quick one, or a quicker two if the pub was close enough. There's one well-known story about Iori visiting the local hospital to entertain the patients at Christmastime. Unfortunately, he arrives late, and as he's walking down the ward, he starts talking to the patients in the beds on either side:

Sorry I'm late. No buses running. I got a lift from an undertaker driving a hearse. I had to sit in the back with the coffin. Talk about a bumpy ride. I told the undertaker, I said, 'Listen here,' I said. 'I don't want to sound ungrateful, but it was a hell of a rough ride back there.' 'Well,' he said, 'you're the first one who's complained.'

Sioni and Iori became well known for their many appearances on a Welsh comedy radio series similar to *Welsh Rarebit*, recorded in the Hall in Cross Hands, and introduced by Alun Williams, one of the best-known Welsh broadcasters of his day. A quarter of a century later, Alun would return to Cross Hands to introduce a concert sponsored by Jo Jones, the impresario with a fat, Lew Grade-style cigar jammed permanently in his mouth, who had established the Cambrian recording company in Pontardawe. If the hall in Cross Hands was full for the Trwpadŵrs, it overflowed the night Alun Williams introduced the television stars of the day: Tony and Aloma, Margaret Williams, Bryn Williams, Janice Thomas, the Hennessys, and, top of the bill, Ryan and Ronnie in their velvet suits, singing 'Green, Green Grass of Home' to the accompaniment of an old Welsh air, usually played on the harp, but played that evening on the piano with great gusto by Alun Williams himself.

Back in the 1950s, Ronnie and Eryl used to slap on the Brylcreem on a Saturday night and go down to the Hall to watch the girls from Gorslas, Tumble, Pontyberem and Dre-fach strutting their stuff on the 'monkey parade' before going into the hall to jive to the rock and roll sounds of Bryn Williams' band from Ammanford. According to one of his school friends, Ronnie was never short of admirers, and one Saturday evening he was seen walking hand in hand with one of the girls down the road from the Cross to a more secluded part of the village, accompanied by one of his mates carrying an umbrella. And what was the role of said friend? It was raining at the time, so somebody had to stand there keeping Ronnie and his girl dry while they proceeded to kiss and cuddle. Ronnie had an eye for the girls from an early age, and it seems that he was far more of an attraction on a Saturday night than Bryn and his Ammanford rockers.

A year before Ryan left Llanfyllin Secondary School, Ronnie had already parted company with Gwendraeth Grammar to work as a clerk in the council offices in Carmarthen. He didn't stay long, and left to join the *South Wales Guardian* newspaper for the princely sum of one pound and ten shillings a week. He looked after the Births, Marriages and Deaths column, or Hatch, Match and Dispatch as it was known by the hardened hacks. Three months later, he was on the move again.

> I soon realised I wasn't cut out to be a journalist. I spent most of my time in funerals, and by the end, I was laughing so much I couldn't see through my tears to write the copy.

So he hopped on a James Brothers' bus from Ammanford and became a conductor, for eleven pounds a week. The late Dafydd Rowlands – poet, scriptwriter and former archdruid – knew Ronnie well, and heard him talk about this work later on:

> He often recalled tales about his experiences on the 'Jimmys', which ran between the Aman and Tawe valleys. I'm sure Ronnie learned a lot about comedy dialogue through engaging in light-hearted banter with the various characters on the buses. A conductor on that route would have to be ready with a quick reply and a sharp wit, and be prepared to amuse the customers with a joke or two. Some of the conductors were natural entertainers, and trips between Glynmoch flats and Lower Cwmtwrch could be absolutely hilarious.

According to his mother's niece Margaret, Ronnie was very happy on the buses. When it was busy he'd have fun with the passengers, pulling their legs and telling jokes. Then during the quiet spells, he'd sit in the back of the bus and write patter spots for his father's double act with Sioni, or sketches for Gwyn D. Evans' concert party, like this one:

So, there was this guy from Cwmtwrch, see, he wanted to go on a train to India. He went to the ticket office and he was told he could only buy a ticket to Cardiff. So, in Cardiff, he went to the ticket office and he was told he could only buy a ticket to London, and then he'd have to buy another one in London which took him to Paris, and so on. By the time he got to Delhi, he'd bought fifty-seven tickets. Fifty-seven! Anyway, he stayed in Delhi for a week, then decided to go home. He was dreading it. All those tickets … Anyway, he went to the ticket office in Delhi and the man asked him where he was going. He said Cwmtwrch. And the man said 'Upper or Lower? Glynmoch flats next stop!'

Once he'd saved enough money working as a bus conductor, Ronnie left the close-knit community of Cefneithin for Cardiff, and the life of a student at the Royal College of Music and Drama. He was one step closer to fulfilling his dream.

Ryan – national service and college

'Swing those arms or I'll tear 'em orff and 'it you with the soggy end.'

'Do you 'ave a mother, airman?'
'Yes, corporal!'
'Then 'ow the 'ell did she manage to produce an ugly turd like you?'

'Am I 'urting you, airman?'
'No, sir!'
'Well, I bloody well ought to be. I'm standing on your bloody 'air. Get that 'air cut!'

'You are fucking useless, airman. What are you?'
'I am a fucking useless airman, corporal.'

Cruel words, spat with malice at eighteen-year-old Thomas Ryan Davies from Llanfyllin, after his first experience of square-bashing. They were noted by John P. Davies, who kept a detailed diary of the time he spent with Ryan in Hut 159 at the Padgate barracks while they were receiving their training. According to John Davies, there were eighteen boys in Hut 159, and he remembers that when Ryan was asked for his name on the first day, his answer was 'I'm Thomas Ryan Davies, but you can call me Twm.' And we did, many years later, when he played a character of that name in one of the most successful Welsh-language situation comedy series ever, *Fo a Fe*, about feuding fathers-in-law from north and south Wales.

The sole purpose of the corporal's humiliating exercise was to turn inexperienced, naïve young men into disciplined machines. Screaming obscenities at the recruits, dehumanising and bullying them, was meant to ensure that they would learn to surrender unquestioningly to the corporal's orders. The boys were expected to exist on a wage of one pound a week, so it wasn't surprising that the food parcels that arrived at the camp from Llanfyllin were given a warm welcome, especially if there was an envelope inside the parcel containing a ten-shilling note. The only place such riches could be spent was in the NAAFI (Navy, Army and Air Force Institution), which was basically a café, a shop and a concert hall with a purpose-built stage all rolled into one.

Ryan was very popular with the other young men because of his natural performing abilities, especially on the NAAFI piano. He could whistle better than any blackbird, and his interpretation of the popular Welsh love song 'Myfanwy' was packed with emotion, and sure to bring a tear to the eye. Long before his successful comedy partnership with Ronnie, Ryan performed on the NAAFI stage in a comedy double act with Pat Durkin, another recruit. Ryan, like Stan Laurel, had a frail, thin body, and he could impersonate Stan perfectly by simply closing his eyes very tightly, pretending he was brokenhearted, and then opening them to take a wide-eyed look at the world like an innocent child. Pat, on the other hand, was large and rotund, and with his small black moustache and wearing a bowler hat, he looked exactly like Oliver Hardy. At half past ten on the dot, the NAAFI door would open, and the corporal would shout his nightly announcement, 'The Queen!' as if her majesty was waiting patiently outside, ready to come in and say 'Good night, boys. Sleep tight,' like Ruth Madoc in

Hi-de-Hi! Then it was Ryan's turn once again. The corporal would shout 'The anthems!' and Ryan would accompany the boys while they sang 'God Save the Queen' and 'Hen Wlad fy Nhadau'. When the last note had been sung, and the corporal had disappeared into the night, the singing would restart with another version of the English national anthem sung in Welsh. The translation touches on the contempt and dislike the recruits felt for their officers: 'Damn the nasty, angry corporals and sergeants. A bunch of horrible individuals. Let's give them the two-finger salute as we shout "Up yours!"'

Throughout this period, in spite of the distance between them, Ryan and his girlfriend Irene were still very close. Every weekend, Ryan would hitchhike from Padgate to Manchester, where Irene was a student at Didsbury College. Irene remembers that they visited the cinema quite often, and that the warmth of the YMCA hostel in the city was far more inviting than the narrow, uncomfortable bed in Hut 159.

The three most hated words in the camp were 'kit inspection' and 'manoeuvres'. Ryan would stand to attention by the side of his bed, at the foot of which were two blankets and two white towels, all folded. In front of him on the floor was a pair of black leather hobnailed boots, smooth to the touch as a result of rubbing candlewax on the leather with the back of a spoon. The leather was then polished further with a mixture of Kiwi polish and spit on a piece of cloth until you could see the face of the corporal staring up at you from the left toecap. Also on the bed, there was a metal cup, a knife, fork and spoon, tinned food and a small white packet containing needles and cotton, soap, a toothbrush and a comb. Slowly, the inspection committee would prowl around like tigers stalking their prey. Then, suddenly, without warning, one of the tigers would jump on an unsuspecting recruit, take one scornful look at the collection of items on the bed, smile sadistically, and throw the lot on the floor.

It was while on manoeuvres that Ryan learned how to use, dismantle and clean a .303 rifle. He practised killing the enemy by attaching a bayonet to the barrel, charging towards a sack full of hay and sticking the bayonet into it with a bloodcurdling scream. He learned survival techniques by spending days in wet, cold tents in atrocious weather that would have definitely exacerbated his asthma. Two years after being called up, Ryan left the RAF and became a mature student at the Normal College in Bangor. In his own words, this was an important turning point in his life:

I started taking things more seriously, and I experienced the thrill of performing in front of a live audience. I'd matured, and I enjoyed being in the company of people who shared my interest in drama, music, composing and performing.

Ryan's fellow students still talk about his many talents, his performances in pubs, on stage, or standing on a table in the George Hotel on the banks of the Menai, whistling 'In a Monastery Garden' far better than Ronnie Ronald, the big radio star of the late fifties who performed it originally. Ryan also made several appearances in concerts in local village halls and acted whenever the opportunity arose. But no mention is ever made of his academic prowess, so who knows how he found time to study at all. He must have done so, because after studying English, Health Education, Music and Dramatic Art Technique under the watchful eye of Principal Richard Thomas, or Dic Tom the Dictator as he was called, Ryan managed to gain his teaching certificate without too much trouble.

Ryan's best friend in college was Rhydderch Jones. Rhydderch had a round face with a ruddy complexion, long, curly, untidy hair and thick lips which were permanently sucking on a cigarette. That's how I remember him when he was a television producer in the BBC's Light Entertainment Department fifteen years later. He was a gentle, likeable man, who could easily be mistaken for Dylan Thomas, one of his heroes, on a dark night. Ryan and Rhydderch were the Elton John and Bernie Taupin of the Normal College. The first song they co-wrote was a love song to a girl called Gwen Llwyd, which earned them ten shillings and sixpence when it was performed on a youth radio programme from Bangor. The next one was another ballad, this time dedicated to a girl who lived in Paris. The lyrics describe the narrow streets and café bars where a young man is drinking wine at his table, thinking about times past and longing for his girlfriend. Although the girl in the song is called Marie, it was written as a love song to Irene. And whilst there wasn't a crock of gold to provide Rhydderch and Ryan with untold riches for writing their songs, they did receive plenty of commissions from the BBC's light entertainment producers for pop songs in the same vein as 'Marie' and 'Gwen Llwyd', and a cheque for ten and six was not to be sniffed at, especially by impoverished students who liked to have a good time in the popular Antelope pub.

The Normal College was situated near the BBC studios in Bangor, and Ryan and Rhydderch were fortunate enough to meet the BBC's representative in Bangor at the time, Sam Jones, who was one of the most influential pioneers in the history of Welsh-language broadcasting, especially in the field of light entertainment. He brought amateur entertainment from the village hall into the radio studio. He discovered Meredydd Evans, Robin Jones and Cledwyn Jones, who became household names in the 1940s as Triawd y Coleg (the College Trio). Sam Jones knew what his audience wanted. In his biography, R. Alun Evans writes of him:

He knew instinctively what his audience would enjoy. He knew that students were more daring than most, and that the audience would be happy to allow them the freedom to express themselves. He had a gift for discovering new talent that would appeal to his audience.

Time after time, people talked about Sam Jones' enthusiasm, his stamina, imagination and vision, words that aptly describe Ryan as well, who was one among many of a whole generation that was hugely influenced by Sam. Ryan and Rhydderch were inspired not only to write more songs, but also to establish a concert party and a three-part harmony trio in the college. Ryan would sing, play the harp and the piano, and his ability to remember a piece of music and play it from memory, having heard it only once, never ceased to amaze his friends. Rhydderch told a story about himself and Ryan going to the cinema in Bangor to see a film called *The Glass Mountain*, starring Michael Denison and Dulcie Gray. According to Rhydderch, it was a terrible film, but the theme music made it into a box office hit. Ryan was thrilled when he heard Nino Rota's score, and when they got to Kit Rose's café in Upper Bangor thirty minutes later, Ryan sat down at the piano and played the theme music in its entirety. Another person who had an important influence on Ryan's future career was Edwin Williams, head of the college's drama department, who looked like a retired army colonel Acccording to J. O. Roberts, another ex-Normal student, who became a very well-known actor himself:

Edwin Williams was tall, and was a gentleman in his dress and his behaviour. And although his moustache gave the impression that he could be sarcastic at times, he was a kind man of great humour, and an accomplished director.

One of the plays he directed was *Noah*, originally written in French by André Obey and translated into Welsh by F. G. Fisher, who established Theatr Fach Llangefni (Llangefni Little Theatre) in Anglesey. Rhydderch Jones played Noah and Ryan played one of his sons, Ham. For the scene where Noah sends out a dove to look for signs that the floods have abated and the water levels fallen, a pigeon from the wilds of Anglesey was shot. But because of the hot summer that year, by the time the pigeon-dressed-as-a-dove was ready to exit the ark, it stank to high heaven. In the play, Noah opens the door, holds the bird aloft, and with the words 'Go my little dove – go on your way', lets it fly out through the window. Since this particular bird was dead, it could not fly, so it had been arranged that the captain of the college rugby team would catch it in the wings before it fell and hit the floor.

Unfortunately, on this particular evening, the bird slipped through his hands like a muddy rugby ball and hit the stage, making a noise that could only be described as a resounding fart. Actors and audience alike were in stitches.

Ryan was always chosen by Edwin Williams for the leading roles in college plays, and he received glowing reviews. 'An exceptional performance,' said one theatre critic about his interpretation of the role of Valère in *Tartuffe* by Molière, and his turn as Thomas Mendip in Christopher Fry's *The Lady's Not for Burning* was similarly praised. Under Edwin Williams' guidance, he learned about the history of theatre and received technical training in speech and movement. Although Ryan was studying to be a teacher, Edwin was completely convinced that he was a professional actor in the making, and that an extra year in the Central School of Speech and Drama to hone his craft would stand him in good stead. Less than six years later, Ryan proved this instinct correct when he left the teaching post in Croydon that he had taken after leaving college, and joined the BBC.

Ronnie – college and early career

When Ronnie and his friend Peter King were told that they, like the female students at the Cardiff College of Music and Drama, were expected to wear leotards in the movement classes, Ronnie's brief reply was unequivocal: 'Men from Cefneithin don't wear tights.' But as we shall see, he did, with hilarious results.

At the time, the college was part of Cardiff Castle, and all the classes were held in rooms designed by William Burgess at the request of the Marquis of Bute. I wonder if Ronnie had the same feeling in 1958 as I did three years later when I crossed the drawbridge and became a student at the castle. Surrounded by Burgess' colourful designs, combining pastel pinks and lime greens, it was impossible not to feel like an extra on a film set being shot by Walt Disney. Solid oak floors, windows with panes of coloured glass, marble pillars, wood panels carved and guilded, walls painted with tasteful murals of Victorian imagery, side by side with characters from ancient Welsh legends, were all watched over by golden cherubs in flight. Inside the castle walls, described as 'the most successful of all the castles of the nineteenth century', were manicured lawns and low stone walls, where it was easy for a young energetic drama student with rapier in hand to imagine that he was Douglas Fairbanks Junior fighting to the death on a black and white cinema screen with Errol Flynn. But unlike Douglas, Ronnie wasn't a tights man, and he didn't feel comfortable prancing around a rehearsal room. Moving gracefully like a latterday Nijinsky wasn't his forte. According to one source, he had surgery on his feet when he was very young, to try and cure his pigeon toes, so he found running and jumping very difficult. However, Ronnie turned his aversion to the balletic garment to his own comedic advantage. In a pair of black tights, and with his friend Peter King similarly attired, they performed a dance which poked fun at the world of the ballet dancer, while at the same time paying homage to Max Wall, one of the most popular comedians of the day, who used to scuttle across the stage wearing a pair of black tights which covered his spindly spider legs. He also wore a small black jacket and sported a Richard III hairstyle down to his shoulders, with a bald pate. His long arms dragged across the floor, and with his backside in the air he looked like a monkey about to mate. No-one noticed Ronnie's feet, and he and his friend received high praise for their inventive choreography.

Students from the castle visited various schools throughout Wales with college productions of well-known plays, and Brian Roberts, who was a pupil in Aberdyfi School, remembers Ronnie as a cast member of two of those productions: *The Diary of Anne Frank* and *Under Milk Wood*. He was so impressed with Ronnie's performances as Organ Morgan and Butcher Beynon that he decided he wanted to be a drama student in Cardiff too. After completing the two-year drama course, he joined the BBC and enjoyed a long career in television drama productions, thanks in the main to Ronnie. The principal of the college, Raymond Edwards, had established a close working relationship with the BBC in Park Place at that time. He was a regular contributor, and was therefore more than happy to release Ronnie to take part in radio plays. Graham Jones, a fellow student who later became a television producer with HTV, remembers Ronnie as a young man who had a far more mature attitude to life than his fellow students because of the time he had spent working as a journalist and as a bus conductor. He was also a dedicated follower of fashion. According to Graham, 'He liked to look smart, in a blazer with a collar and tie, and a grey scarf.'

The girls enjoyed his company, and Lenna Pritchard Jones, who co-presented a satirical programme on BBC Wales with Ronnie in the late 1960s, remembers him asking one of the girls in the college for a date. The girl agreed on the condition that Ronnie would go with her to a Pentecostal church service at the City Temple in Cardiff on Sunday night. Ronnie and Lenna were sharing a flat at the time, and the matter was discussed thoroughly. Finally, Ronnie said that he would go if Lenna went too. When she asked him why he wanted her to tag along, he said with a cheeky grin, 'If you're with me, Lenna, she won't try and save me.' A good example, according to Lenna, of his dry wit: 'He was a very humorous, likeable boy. Someone you'd be quite happy to have as a brother.'

Einir Wyn Hughes, who shared the flat in Ilton Road with Ronnie and Lenna, went one step further and decided that she would be happy to have Ronnie as her husband. The landlord and landlady, Mr and Mrs Davies, always extended a warm welcome to music and drama students, having been members of the Glanaman opera company themselves years before. Einir was a music student, and she and Ronnie were in such close harmony that, six months after arriving in Cardiff, they were engaged. The ring Ronnie bought cost him £24, which was a lot of money at that time. He was always one for the grand financial gesture, and this would land him in trouble more than once over the years. After they got married in 1961, Einir left college to work for Anglo Autos while Ronnie shared his time between a tiling company and the BBC drama studios in Park Place. But he had other ideas as well.

He saw himself as a film director and producer, and his dream came true with financial support from his parents May and Iori, who were far too willing to rescue their son from more than one financial disaster over the years, according to his sister Rhoda. His college friend Graham and Lyn Jones, who established the Wales Production Company with Ryan and Ronnie in the 1970s, believed that Ronnie had always been drawn towards the world of the director, producer and writer rather than the actor and performer. So with his parents' help and heavy financial backing from businessmen in Pontyberem who knew the family, and thought they knew Ronnie, he started Dyffryn Films. He rented two rooms in the Phoenix building in the dockland area of Cardiff, one room for him, and the other for a young film editor, Robin Rollinson, who in later years became one of the directors of *Pobol y Cwm*.

It could be argued that Ronnie was the first independent film director in Wales, working for Welsh-language television twenty years before S4C was established. In fact, his son Arwel told me that his description of himself on his passport at the time was: 'Managing Director, Dyffryn Films'. It conjures up a picture of Ronnie with a fat cigar in his mouth, sitting behind a solid wooden desk in a black leather chair, with a Jaguar outside the window. Indeed, that part of the dream came true for a while during the Ryan and Ronnie years, but not as a result of establishing Dyffryn Films.

Robin Rollinson has a very hazy recollection of the films made by Ronnie in the early days of Dyffryn Films, but he does remember a light-hearted film Ronnie made for the daily magazine programme *Heddiw*. Newport Council had put a new one-way system in place, and one of the programme's producers had discovered that, although it was illegal to drive up the one-way system in a car, no mention was made of animals. Shortly thereafter, Ronnie was seen riding up that very street against the flow of traffic on the back of a very confused camel. The film still exists in the BBC archives, unlike some of the television shows Ryan and Ronnie recorded, which have since disappeared. He also made a film about the Gilbern – the Welsh sports car that was built in Llantwit Fardre, near Pontypridd. The Dyffryn Films office was dangerously close to some well-established pubs in the docks area – the Dowlais, the Old Bute Dock, the Packet and the Ship and Pilot. Ronnie spent many an afternoon socialising with the clientele of these pubs, and creating a very successful career for himself in the film industry – on paper. Ronnie was never short of ideas, but he wasn't as successful in turning those ideas into completed films.

One of his more ambitious projects was *A Stranger in the City*, a pilot film scripted, directed and produced by Ronnie. His plan was to shoot one episode, show it to the BBC and hope that they were prepared to commission a whole series based on it. The story was about a young boy, Ronnie perhaps, coming to Cardiff and having to face many problems and temptations. Graham Jones, Ronnie's friend, played an inexperienced student meeting the minister of a Cardiff chapel in Bute Park who tries to seduce him. To show such a scene in Wales in the 1960s would have caused an uproar, especially considering the homophobic attitude of the time, and the illegality of homosexual practices. One scene was shot outside the Hayes Island Snack Bar in the middle of the city, and Ronnie payed a location fee of £100, the equivalent of £1,800 today. No small independent film company would even entertain the idea of squandering such a large amount of the budget on one location now, but this was another example of Ronnie playing the Hollywood director on the streets of Cardiff. The all-important pilot was shown to the BBC, and they decided not to commission a series based on the one episode. Dyffryn Films was a failure. Each one of Ronnie's business ventures over the years was a failure, without exception. With his engaging smile and his gift of the gab, he could persuade friends, family and unsuspecting business people alike that investing a substantial sum in his latest venture, usually a pub, would be a good idea. It never was. Why? Because the idea of being the owner of a successful business appealed to him, but he was never prepared to work hard enough to make it succeed. It's also true to say that Ronnie was too kind to be a tough businessman, and over the years, many people took advantage of his generous nature.

While he was trying to get work for Dyffryn Films, he also appeared on television and radio. He presented schools programmes for the BBC's Education Department, and a television series for young people called, aptly enough, *Youth Club*. He also read the news in Welsh and English and worked as a voiceover artist. His talents were many and varied, and he felt that some of those talents deserved better financial recognition, especially his work as a radio actor. To this end, he wrote a memo to the Head of Contracts, Iris Evans. He was offered a raise, and his tongue-in-cheek reply is still kept in the BBC archives in Caversham.

Dear Miss Evans,

Thank you for your letter of 14 February 1963 in which you informed me of the reviewing of my drama fee from six guineas to eight. It is, of course, wonderful news, and I am grateful that you were able to authorise this increase. I'm sure you'll be glad to know that I can now buy all my children shoes and stockings, and perhaps pay the poor grocer round the corner. I may even be able to get the the furniture back so that my poor wife can have a sit down for a change.

Seriously, my humble thanks and assurances that your action is indeed greatly appreciated.

Kind regards, Ronnie Williams

Humility was not one of Ronnie's character traits, and it's clear that this letter was written by someone who believed at the time, as he did throughout his life, that he never received the recognition he deserved for his work as an actor and a writer.

Although Ronnie and Ryan formed their partnership in 1967, the pair had met seven years previously. While Ryan was teaching in London, he would travel to Cardiff to appear on radio and television programmes occasionally. He and Ronnie met during one of these visits, when Ronnie was presenting *Youth Club* and Ryan was singing songs at the piano.

Despite the failure of Dyffryn Films, Ronnie was very busy presenting on television, acting on radio, reading news bulletins in Welsh and English and working as a television continuity announcer. He was also an early celebrity in Wales, and he was in great demand throughout the country, regularly opening events and officiating at launches.

In 1963, Ronnie, Einir and their newborn son Arwel were living in Cardiff, and a year later they got a lodger – a young man from Anglesey who had joined the BBC in October of that year. I remember that the family lived in 14 Lôn-y-mynydd, Rhiwbina, but how I became a lodger there, I honestly can't recall. After leaving the Royal College of Music and Drama, where Ronnie had studied before me, I had joined the daily television magazine programme *Heddiw*. I would see Ronnie in the canteen in Broadway, where the television studios were located at the time. Perhaps he offered me lodgings over a cup of tea there, or more likely after a pint later on at the BBC Club on Newport Road. Einir can't remember either how she was foolish enough to share her house with a young lad who wouldn't stop eating. She claims that, late at night, I would go downstairs to the kitchen and cook myself a meal. I do remember carrying a load of bricks and planks up to my room to build some rickety shelves for my books, and also that Mrs Bower, who lived across the road, didn't take to me at all because I kept parking my white Triumph Herald in front of her house. My friendship with Ronnie gave me the opportunity to start writing topical songs for a programme called *Stiwdio B*, one of BBC Wales' most pioneering comedy programmes of the time, presented by Ronnie and Lenna Pritchard Jones. Two years previously, David Frost had greeted television audiences with a smirk and a 'Hello, good evening and welcome', as the presenter of the groundbreaking *That Was the Week That Was*, which gave politicians and establishment figures a weekly kick up the backside with a smile, a song and a satirical sketch. John Cleese, Peter Cook, Richard Ingrams, John Bird, John Betjeman, Kenneth Tynan and even Roald Dahl could all be called upon to stick a thorn in the side of the government of the day.

Two years after that, *Stiwdio B* put the Welsh establishment under the microscope and looked satirically at the world in general. 1965 was a good year for satirists. Ian Smith declared Rhodesia's independence, and Ronnie Biggs, the great train robber, escaped from Wandsworth prison. Alec Douglas-Home resigned as the leader of the Conservative Party and Kenneth Tynan was the first person to use the F-word on television. Another four-letter word which was given a lot of publicity in 1965 was 'fags', when cigarette companies were banned from advertising on television. As one of the contributors to *Stiwdio B*, I remember using the ban as a hook for a song about a Welsh tobacco called Amlwch Shag, but the song never made it to the programme, more than likely because of the tobacco's dubious name.

One of the memorable characters created for *Stiwdio B* was Ifans, a bigoted, opinionated, Alf Garnett-type north Walian who wore a black homburg and a shirt with a Jesus collar. He walked with a limp and pushed a large handcart, which he leaned on for his weekly monologue, usually aimed at establishments such as the Inland Revenue, which he referred to as the England Revenue, or the English government, who were always treating us badly, according to Ifans. Why? Because he maintained that 'Britannia Rules the Wales'. According to one television critic, 'The writing doesn't sparkle, and the acting needs to be sharper.' However, he had some kind words about Ronnie's performance, and the fact that he had developed into a very competent impersonator. When the make-up department put Brylcreem in Ronnie's hair, combed it straight across his forehead and added a pair of black-framed glasses, he became the Right Honourable Cledwyn Hughes, Secretary of State for Wales.

Ronnie's next role, in a co-production between the BBC and the National Theatre Company called *Through the Door of Hope*, took him from the world of television comedy to the stage of the National Eisteddfod Pavilion, where he played the role of Daniel, a young farmer leaving Wales to look for a better life in South America. This was a serious drama, but the play, which told the story of how the *Mimosa* sailed from Liverpool to Patagonia in 1865, and especially the scenes depicting the Welsh settlers fighting to come to terms with the harsh reality of life in a barren land, had its funny moments. In one scene, the settlers were ploughing the soil and sowing seed. One actor with a sack full of imaginary seeds on his back was sowing with gusto, arms flailing like a windmill out of control. In a loud stage whisper, one of the other actors was heard to say, 'For God's sake, Ifan, don't sow over here, I haven't ploughed that bit yet.' The following night, proper seeds were used, and a fair few of the 'settlers' slipped on their way from one side of the stage to the other.

By 1965, Ronnie was a well-known media figure in Wales. Ryan, meantime, was about to leave his teaching job in Croydon, move to Cardiff and join the BBC. But let's have a look at his London years before that.

Ryan and the London Welsh

L ondon was a Mecca for young people from Wales in the 1960s. There had been a long history of migration to the English capital dating back to the nineteenth century, when farmers from rural areas moved there to start dairy enterprises. Ryan enrolled in the Central School of Speech and Drama in 1959 before beginning his teaching career one year later in Croydon. At the time, 70 per cent of teachers in London came from Wales. Another one of these was Hafina Clwyd, a prominent London Welsh girl from Denbigh, and a close friend of Ryan. Hafina kept a diary which gives us a vivid insight into the life of the London Welsh community between 1957 and 1964. There are frequent references to Ryan, the first in August 1959 when Ryan and his close friend Rhydderch were performing with members of the London Welsh Drama Society in an eisteddfod in Caernarfon, north Wales. The pavilion was full to overflowing, and amongst the audience that evening was Caradog Pritchard, three-time winner of the bardic crown and a major literary figure in Wales. Sitting next to him was his wife Matti, a formidable London Welsh socialite, with their dog Benji on her lap. When Ryan came on stage dressed as a bespectacled, nervous, bowler-hatted gentleman with a wing collar and black tie, and proceeded to mime eating chips in an imaginary chip shop, Benji decided to show his appreciation of Ryan's performance by jumping on stage and barking for his attention. Ryan stopped his act, knelt on one knee and started talking to the dog, which then barked in all the right places, as if he understood what Ryan was saying, and Ryan reacted as if he understood Benji's comments. According to Hafina's diary, the audience was in stiches, and Ryan and Benji's unrehearsed double act was the highlight of the evening.

The London Welsh drama cast regularly won the drama competition in the Eisteddfod. They won in 1960, with Ryan in the main part, and then entertained the audience with a variety show. It started in a seemingly traditional way. As the curtain slowly opened, Ryan was playing the Welsh National Anthem on the piano with dignity and passion, and as a mark of respect, the audience got up from their seats. Having got them there, Ryan moved up a musical gear, and the anthem became an uptempo song, with the words urging the audience to sit down and enjoy the show. This time, Hafina's diary records that the embarrassed audience sat down, laughing, clapping and thoroughly enjoying the fact that Ryan had caught them out.

The London Welsh had their own lively club in Gray's Inn Road, where they held a dance every Saturday night, and drama and choir rehearsals during the week. It was also the birthplace of the concert party Y Tri Taff (the three Taffs): Ryan, his cousin Alun and his friend Bryn Richards. Ryan was the driving force behind it, and, according to Bryn:

> He expected perfection on stage, whether we were acting or singing. If you forgot your lines, he'd let you know that he wasn't happy in no uncertain terms. Only the highest standard was good enough. He was a perfectionist.

The Tri Taff recorded songs that Ryan and Rhydderch had written, on the Delyse record label, and they appeared on television when BBC Wales started broadcasting in 1964. It's obvious from the entries in Hafina's diary that she and the Gray's Inn Road crowd knew how to enjoy themselves. She refers to a party held at Caradog and Matti Pritchard's home on 4 November 1959, a month after Ryan had started as a student at the Central College. It was a more sedate affair, perhaps, than other parties being held at the time in swinging London, but nevertheless, two people at least were intent on having a good time.

> Ryan and Rhydderch spent the evening trying to impress Isabella Wallich, the woman who founded the Delyse record label. She is an Italian lady who is very interested in recording songs in the Welsh language. They followed her round the room singing 'O, Isabella'. It was an evening given over to singing, eating *cawl* and pleasing Isabella.

At another Matti Pritchard extravaganza, Ryan was introduced to Maria Korchinska, a harpist and a friend of Isabella's. Having listened to Ryan and Rhydderch singing to the accompaniment of a small harp, she turned to Ryan and told him in her thick Russian accent 'You harrr hay hinterestink yong man – but you cannot play ze 'arp!' Be that as it may, Ryan and Rhydderch made a record called *Welsh Fireside Songs* on Delyse. The words were written by famous Welsh poets and set to old Welsh airs played on 'ze 'arp' by Maria. No doubt the sentimental sleevenotes would have tugged at the heartstrings of Welsh emigrants:

> This selection of songs is an attempt to evoke the warm glow of a Welsh hearth in one of the lonely moorland or hill homesteads of the hinterland. For it was such an environment that gave them birth, and it is there that they have flourished since time immemorial. The two young singers, Rhydderch Jones and Ryan Davies, are popular exponents of this art form.

Ryan and Rhydderch were in great demand, especially by the Welsh chapels in Charing Cross, King's Cross, Harrow and Finchley. One evening, while trying to explain bilingually how intricate singing with the harp could be, Rhydderch got lost in translation. Ryan had already sat on the stool with the harp facing the wrong way, which was a part of their act. As Ryan turned the harp the right way, Rhydderch began his off-the-cuff explanation:

> He plays one hair on the 'arp, and then I count and I come in with my own hair. But the hair that he's playing and the hair that I am singing are not the same hairs, but they fit, and we finish together. So ... um ... er ...

Ryan could see that Rhydderch was trudging bravely through linguistic quicksand, and came to his assistance: 'So it's everybody for himself in the middle and God help everybody at the end.' The audience loved the original presentation and quirky explanation, and Ryan kept it in the act. They also appeared on BBC television and on the Welsh commercial station TWW (Television Wales and the West). Princess Alexandra was in the audience when they sang for the first time in the Albert Hall, and Ryan first delivered his famous one-liner: 'Ladies and gentlemen. I'd like to thank you all for coming, and I'd like to thank Albert for the loan of his hall.'

Ryan and Rhydderch were very close, and Hafina's diary reveals that they not only shared the flat with Huwcyn, another ex-Normal College student, but also the only large bed in the flat:

> It can be very wild there at times. Ryan, unfortunately, sleeps between Huwcyn and Rhydderch, so every time they turn over, Ryan is thrown into the air like a

shuttlecock. I had a party in my flat the other night, and there was quite a crowd there, with Ryan in the middle of it all like the live wire that he is, telling jokes and singing. He should definitely be on the stage. He was still singing when a policeman knocked on the door at two in the morning. The neighbours had obviously complained about the noise. As luck would have it, he was Welsh, and within a few minutes of entering the flat, he had a pint of beer in his hand and was leaning against the piano having a good time like everybody else. If my next-door neighbour had seen him, his thumbs pushing his braces out as he sang at the top of his voice, he'd have lost faith in law and order for ever.

In addition to the diary, Hafina started keeping a visitors' book in September 1960. By February 1961, over two hundred people had accepted her hospitality, and there was also a constant flow of Welsh musical talent into the London Welsh Club. One year, she notes that amongst the visitors were the Treorchy Male Choir, Gwyneth Jones, the opera singer and school friend of Ryan's, a quartet and a choir from north Wales, all taking part in a concert introduced by one of Wales' most famous actors, Siân Phillips.

Since Ryan spent so much of his time performing in concerts all over London as well as travelling back to Wales to appear on television and radio, one could easily forget that he did all his performing in his spare time after a full day's teaching at St John's School in Shirley, near Croydon. According to Margaret Lewis, the widow of the headmaster Gerallt Lewis, Ryan was a hard worker and an inspired teacher, who believed stongly in discipline. Ryan and Gerallt had the greatest respect for each other, and the headmaster would quite often supervise Ryan's Friday afternoon lessons so that he could jump on the train to Cardiff and become Ryan Davies, television star.

On 2 April 1961, Ryan attended an event where, for the first time in his life, despite being dressed in a morning suit and tie, he was not the main attraction. The star of the show was Irene, his sweetheart since their school days, in her ivory-coloured satin dress with a large bow at the back at the couple's wedding in Llanrhaedr-ym-Mochnant, the village in Powys where Irene was born. After a five-day honeymoon in the Lake District and a quick visit to his parents' home in Llanfyllin, Ryan was back in London preparing for the next drama production. This time it was to be a translation by Rhydderch of *Offshore Island*, a play by Marghanita Laski. According to Iwan Thomas, a mutual friend:

A meeting was arranged in London and the boys went to the dramatist's flat to discuss the play. The discussion went on for hours, the gins and martinis were knocked back, and eventually they forgot about the play and started discussing Welsh poetry, a subject close to Miss Laski's heart. Ryan noticed an instrument in the corner of the room, and under the influence of too much alcohol, the inevitable happened. Ryan and Rhydderch ended the evening, much to Marghanita's delight, singing Welsh poetry to the accompaniment of the harpsichord.

The following year, the National Eisteddfod was held in Llanelli, and Ryan once again played the starring role in *Charley's Aunt*. The London Welsh company won the drama competition for the third year running. The adjudicator was very complimentary, especially about Ryan's performance:

He knows how to move quickly across the stage, and although he has a variety of expressions, he can speak volumes with one look, and knows the value of the dramatic pause. The farce is his forte, and his comic timing is brilliant.

It is, of course, sheer coincidence that the said adjudicator was none other than Ryan's drama tutor and mentor at the Normal College, Edwin Williams. And to be fair to him, everything that was said about Ryan then would be repeated time and again in the future during his successful career as a professional performer.

However, the London Welsh, and Ryan amongst them, received a roasting in the press by Welsh-language activists at that Eisteddfod, who accused them of being traitors and selling their souls for well-paid jobs in England. Hafina Clwyd, in her weekly column in the Welsh newspaper *Y Faner*, was quick to defend their position:

We stand accused of being traitors, of betraying our country by moving to England. There are a quarter of a millon of us in London. What if we were to return to Wales, wanting a job, a place to live and entertainment? Our accusers tell us that they would rather collect the dole in Wales than earn a living as teachers in England. What a brave sentiment! It shows that they know nothing of living on handouts. I told them to stuff their narrow-minded attitude, and their racism.

Hafina was answered in turn by Neil Jenkins, a prominent activist, who referred to Ryan indirectly:

What did you give us, the cave dwellers, at Llanelli this year? Wesker? Osborne ? No! *Charley's Aunt*. If you believe the Welsh language is merely a medium for farce, you can keep your bloody culture.

Although Hafina defended her fellow Welshmen in London, privately she sympathised with the criticism levelled against them:

There's a lot of truth in what they say, but I won't admit it publicly. I appreciate that Wales needs us back home, to support the culture and the Welsh way of life, and for many of us, it's a dilemma that we face daily.

But despite the criticism, the London Welsh contingent were back in force the following year on the stage of the National Eisteddfod at Llandudno, with Ryan playing a starring role once again, this time as Morgan Llwyd, a Welsh Puritan preacher who came to prominence in the time of Oliver Cromwell. One of the highlights of Eisteddfod week was the London Welsh evening variety show, and in Llandudno an unofficial ceremony was held during one of the sketches, when Rhydderch Jones, dressed as the Archdruid, announced that the bardic chair had been won by someone bearing the pseudonym Eldorado, a popular ice-cream of the day. That fact is crucial to the story.

'Therefore,' intoned Rhydderch in his best Archdruid's voice, 'when the trumpet sounds for the third time, will Eldorado, and only Eldorado, please rise.' The trumpets sounded, the search lights scoured the darkness of the pavilion looking for Eldorado, and finally found the diminutive figure of Ryan, dressed as an usherette, complete with a tray full of ice-cream, shouting: 'Eldorado. Eldorado, darling. Would you like an Eldorado choc ice?' Before the Eldorado's prospective buyer could reach into her handbag, Ryan started backing away as he saw two druids in flowing robes bearing down on him to escort him to the stage to claim his chair. Ryan, however, thought they were going to throw him out for selling the ice-cream, so he dropped his tray and started running across the pavilion, hotly pursued by other druids in their green, blue and white gowns. The audience were in hysterics. Years later, they would see the ice-cream lady again in Ryan and Ronnie's TV series as Phyllis the barmaid, with her blonde beehive hairdo, red stilettos and ready wit.

It's not known whether some of the BBC bosses in Cardiff were in the pavilion to see the show, but soon after the Eisteddfod, it was decided that it was time to bring the talents of Ryan and his London Welsh friends to the small screen. So a musical review was composed, by Ryan of course, and it was the first of its kind in Welsh. It was set in London and was called *Gwanwyn yn y Ddinas* ('Springtime in the City'). The opening sequence showed Ryan standing guard outside Buckingham Palace in a busby two sizes too big for him. Having finished a cigarette which he was smoking on the sly, he breaks into song about the important people who visit the palace. By the end of the song, there's a dreamy, faraway look in his eyes as he starts to imagine that he and his friends in the Tri Taff are wandering the streets of London. Before long, they meet three young ladies who join them in a song-and-dance routine. But the dream soon comes to an end, and Ryan wakes up to find that he is still a guard outside Buckingham Palace, in a busby two sizes too big for him. The London papers raved about the review. The *London Welshman* called it 'a gem of a programme. It showed that, if a real effort is made, something genuinely Welsh can be translated to the sophisticated TV idiom with complete aplomb.' Hafina Clwyd noted in her diary, 'I have heard a rumour that the BBC is going to steal Ryan from us. Dammit!'

And the rumour was true. Meredydd Evans had been appointed as the head of the BBC's new Light Entertainment Department in Cardiff. Although he was a Doctor of Philosophy, and had recently returned to Wales from Princeton University in the USA, everyone knew him as Merêd. In the 1940s, he had been a member of a popular trio on Welsh radio called Triawd y Coleg (the College Trio). He was also a singer and collector of Welsh folk songs, and, after he returned to Wales, he and his wife Phyllis Kinney edited three definitive collections of Welsh folk music. Merêd was aware of Ryan's talent, and after seeing the television review, he decided that Ryan should be the cornerstone of the light entertainment programming. Merêd was a very determined individual, and Geraint Stanley Jones, a former controller of BBC Wales and chief executive of S4C, has no doubt that his contribution to the development of Welsh light entertainment programmes on television was invaluable and innovative: 'He inspired a generation of young people, and laid the foundations for a Welsh-language channel. Without Merêd's vision, I doubt if S4C would ever have been established.'

Those of us who were lucky to be there in those early days felt that we were on a mission, and that under Merêd's charismatic leadership, this mission was not impossible. He could instil in you the feeling that it was us against the world. It was 'Once more unto the breach, dear friends.' It was 'Gwlad, gwlad, pleidiol wyf i'm gwlad,' and we were his people. One of the first programmes on the newly established BBC Wales in 1964 was *Hep! Hep! Hwrê!*, and the viewers saw Ryan and the other two Taffs performing, as well as Russ Jones and his band from Pontarddulais, and six young girls from Cardiff who sang under the name of The Teledis.

TWW came up with a Welsh version of *Mr and Mrs* called *Siôn a Siân*, presented by Dewi Richards and Meriel Griffiths, whose husband Lynn Davies was a future Olympic gold medallist.

Ryan was still a teacher in Croydon, and was appearing occasionally on *Stiwdio B*, the satirical programme which Ronnie was presenting, but as the output from the BBC and TWW in Cardiff increased, Ryan's talents were in greater demand month by month. The writing on the blackboard was clear, and Ryan's days as a teacher were numbered. On 27 September 1965, Merêd launched his weapon of mass entertainment, and Ryan signed a contract with the BBC for £1000, the first contract of its kind in the history of Welsh broadcasting. At last, Ryan Davies and Ronnie Williams were together, working for the BBC. Little did they realise then that, in two years' time, they would become a phenomenon that Wales has never seen the like of, before or since.

'Ladies and gentlemen, please welcome ... Ryan and Ronnie.'

Together for the first time

Exchanging the security of a teaching job for a one-year contract at the BBC was a risky choice for Ryan. He and Irene discussed it at length, and agreed that it was a risk worth taking. After all, he could always return to teaching if the performing wasn't a success. Looking back, and knowing as we do that Ryan was one of the most versatile and talented performers Wales has ever produced, it's difficult to believe that the move had to be dicussed at all. But throughout his career, Ryan always listened to Irene's opinion about any decision he needed to make, respected her advice, and usually accepted it. So by May 1965, Irene, Ryan and their one-year-old daughter Bethan had left London and were living in St. Fagans, on the outskirts of Cardiff. The garage very quickly became Ryan's study, where he composed, read his scripts, relaxed and occasionally doodled on the table. I wonder how much a framed Davies doodle would fetch today!

Bethan remembers that they were the first in the street to own a colour television set and a video recorder, which Ryan used to analyse his own television performances, to see what worked and what didn't. Merêd, the head of the department, was over the moon. The star from Glanaman was to be the captain of a team of professional performers who would be available every day of the week, not just at weekends, as in the days when radio and television in Wales relied on amateur talent. They included Margaret Williams, Bryn Williams, Mari Griffith, Gaynor Morgan Rees, Janice Thomas, and later on Myfanwy Talog and Sue Roderick. They would all in turn appear with Ryan, and later with Ryan and Ronnie in their television series. One of the first series that Ryan co-presented with Charles Williams, a very experienced radio and television actor, gave the villages and towns of Wales an opportunity to show how talented they were, but Ryan's performance was criticised by the television pundits. They mentioned the 'subtlety' of Charles' performance, while Ryan was accused of 'overacting'. His experience on stage with the London Welsh club, which involved large, sweeping movements, did not translate well to the small, intimate television screen. On stage, Ryan had to project in order for facial movements to be seen by the audience. In a studio, a slight upward flick of the eyebrow in close-up could be seen clearly by the audience at home. Television was new. The technique had to be different.

Because television light entertainment was in its infancy in Wales, professional performers were few and far between, and as a result the same faces appeared regularly. Ryan's face was seen more often than most. His lively presentation of a folk-based musical programme called *Hob y Deri Dando* was praised by the press. The audience and the performers sat on bales of hay in a studio which was made-up to look like a barn. The format was old-fashioned, traditional and very popular, unlike the programme that replaced it in 1967. *Disc a Dawn* was a far more modern affair, with pop music replacing the traditional folk tunes. The programme's title translates as 'discs and talent', and in Welsh-speaking Wales in the mid-1960s, both were very rare.

When you experiment with new performers, you sometimes make mistakes, and the big mistake in the first programme was a group calling itself Yours Sincerely. And who were they? Endaf Emlyn, Derek Boote and me. Why the other two agreed to let me join their newly-formed band I shall never know, especially since I played the few chords I knew incorrectly. In hindsight, it reminds me of the famous sketch on the Morecambe and Wise show. Eric's piano playing was criticised by André Previn, the world-famous conductor, who accused him of playing all the wrong notes on the piano. Morecambe grabs Previn by the lapels – a move used often by Ryan and Ronnie – drags him forward until their noses are touching, then delivers the devastating retort: 'Listen, sunshine, I was playing the right notes, but not necessarily in the right order!' Truth be told, on *Disc a Dawn*, I played the wrong chords in the wrong order, and that was my first and last appearance as a rhythm guitarist on the small screen.

However, that was not my last contribution to the programme. Ruth Price, the producer, told Endaf and me to visit the nightclubs of Cardiff to find women who would be prepared to come to the studio and dance to the music on the programme. I remember visiting a club in the Canton area, and trying to slip into the club past a very large, black, threatening bouncer. We explained to our new-found friend that we represented the BBC and worked for a pop programme.

'What sort of a programme is that then, like?'

'It's a Welsh pop programme called *Disc a Dawn*.'

'Discs at dawn,' he said, pronouncing 'dawn' like daybreak. 'Well I'm Welsh, like, and I've never 'eard of it!'

Trying to dance to music which wasn't meant to be danced to, played on acoustic guitars and sung in Welsh, must have been a bizzare experience for the Canton nightclub dancers, who were more at home with the Monkees, the Beach Boys and the Foundations.

Away from the television studio, Ryan was recording an EP on Wren records. It contained a Welsh version of 'Yesterday', a song about the Tal-y-llyn railway and a Welsh song, 'Galw arnaf i', whose opening words are 'Call on me, and I'll come to you'. This describes perfectly Ryan's inevitable response to any producer.

He was never one to refuse work and, years later, when it was suggested to him that he should slow down and take it easy, he never listened. In 1966 alone, he presented two series of *Hob y Deri Dando*, acted in two comedy series and a radio play. He also acted in his first professional role on the stage of the Aberafan National Eisteddfod, and was in great demand all over Wales as a concert compère. 1966 was also the year in which he lost his father. Everyone who saw them together knew how close they were, and William had been an important musical influence on his son. According to Nans, Ryan's mother, 'If Ryan had to be scolded for any reason, I was the one to do that. He never once had a telling-off from his father.'

William Thomas Davies was buried in the cemetery of Hen Fethel chapel, Glanaman, at the foot of the Black Mountain. Little did the family know that they would return to the same place to bury his son, who died far too young only eleven years later.

Another black mountain made the news on 21 October 1966 – the coal tip above the village of Aberfan that slipped and enveloped the village school of Pantglas. I can remember coming home from a filming trip in north Wales, and stopping to look down at the village, not realising why there was so much activity below. Ronnie was the newsreader on duty that day and throughout the night, reading bulletins and updates sent through by reporters from the scene of the tragedy.

Partly because of his appearances on *Studio B*, Ronnie was invited to appear in a satirical show at one of the most memorable National Eisteddfods of the twentieth century, held in Bala, north Wales, in 1967. This summer would come to be known as the Summer of Love, a social phenomenon that occurred when 100,000 young people converged on San Francisco. Those who converged on the Eisteddfod field would remember the summer

Ronnie, his sister Rhoda, and his parents May and Iori

Ronnie as a young student outside the Royal College of Music and Drama, in the grounds of Cardiff Castle

Ronnie and Einir, his first wife, on their wedding day in Llangwm, north Wales, 1961

Ronnie and Einir in London, 1958

Four generations. Arwel, Ronnie's son, with his father, his grandmother, and great-grandfather in 1963

Iori and May with their grandson, Arwel

Ronnie's children, Bethan and Arwel

Ronnie and Iori looking through press cuttings

A rare photograph of the father and son duo

'My name is Ronnie Williams, I'm a director.'

Ronnie during his Dyffryn Films days

The impresario, creating an impression

'Good afternoon.
Our next programme
of popular music begins
at 2.30.'

Presenting the satirical programme *Stiwdio B* before the Ryan and Ronnie days

'Good evening. Here is the news.'

Playing a new role – the manager of the White Lion

Ronnie interviewing Cliff Richard for his television programme *Late Call*

The evergreen members of *Licyris Olsorts,* and Ronnie. From left to right: Glanffrwd James, Martin Griffiths, Morlais Thomas, Ronnie and Elwyn Willimas

Out on manoeuvres as Dan Bach y Blagard in *Licyris Olsorts*

Old at 57

of '67 as the time they first saw Ryan and Ronnie performing together, and creating their own phenomenon in Welsh entertainment and popular culture.

According to the historian Dr John Davies, 'In the mid-1960s, Welsh-language entertainment moved almost overnight into the pub, or perhaps I should say back into the pub, another testimony to the deep-seated love the Welsh have for beer.' Every night during Eisteddfod week, the streets of Bala were awash with drink and drunkards. According to one irate letter writer in the press, speaking directly to the young people at the festival:

> You are so arrogant with your glasses, your infernal noise, and your non-stop drinking. Gangs of you inside and outside on the pavement, so that there was no room to pass. Your behaviour was intolerable.

Archdruid Gwyndaf, with all the authority at his disposal, stood on the main stone of the Gorsedd Circle, and proclaimed: 'I hope we have dry weather – and a dry Eisteddfod.'

But it was not to be. There was trouble at the White Lion. Tawe Griffith, who conducted the singing at every Eisteddfod, was leading a hastily formed choir when a rowdy crowd from west Wales decided to turn up and spoil the party. The *Daily Post* was quick to condemn their behaviour, but I. B.Griffith, one of the team of television reporters at the Eisteddfod, came to their defence: 'The lads inside the White Lion, singing their hymns and drinking their beer, are merely enjoying themselves.'

Perhaps it was after one such night of heavy drinking that somebody decided to put an end once and for all to the nearby cockerel's early morning call at the tented village which had been erected on the outskirts of the Eisteddfod field. According to people who stayed there, everbody was behaving completely irresponsibly. When the singing and drinking in town eventually came to an end at about five o'clock in the morning, and campers had crawled into their sleeping bags for a few hours' sleep, the crowing would begin. Finally, someone silenced the cockerel by depriving him of his feathers, one by one, while he was still alive.

The Eisteddfod of 1967 is remembered by some as the festival where a group called Y Blew performed, and created a little bit of history for themselves by being the first Welsh-language pop group to play electric guitars. The chairman of the Literary Committee had invited the group to join other pop groups of the day in the Literary Pavilion – the poets' holy of holies. One or two protested, but their objections were drowned out by the guitar playing of Richard Lloyd, the organ playing of Dave Williams, Geraint Evans' drumming, Maldwyn Pate's lead vocal and the bass playing of Dafydd Evans, son of the politician Gwynfor Evans, who had won the Plaid Cymru seat for Carmarthen the previous year. Y Blew didn't have much in common with the other groups who shared the stage with them. They were 'too nice-nice and old-fashioned', and Dafydd Evans felt that the youth of Wales should be dancing to a different tune.

> It's high time someone started screaming in bad Welsh,
> for the sake of those young people who have never heard
> songs in their own language like the ones sung by the
> Beatles and the Rolling Stones.

One of the most colourful characters in the history of the National Eisteddfod was Sir Albert Cynan Evans-Jones CBE, who was better known by his bardic name, Cynan. He was the only person ever to be elected to the position of Archdruid for a second term. He was also responsible for designing the modern ceremonies of the Crowning and Chairing of the Bard. He was a large gentleman, with a rotund body and a round face. In fact, Cynan looked quite like Billy Cotton, the band leader and entertainer, and like Billy, he was a showman. Although his second term as Archdruid had ended the previous year, Cynan made headline news on the Eisteddfod field in 1967. His private life was given prominence in the satirical magazine *Lol*, the scourge of the Welsh establishment, of which Cynan was a fully paid-up member. One of the pictures in the magazine was of a nude young lady by the name of Shan, with the word 'Censor' stamped across her breasts – a pretty unsubtle reference to the former Archdruid, who had recently been appointed as the critical reader of any plays published in the Welsh language. In addition to 'Censor', three other words could be seen in the picture, much lower down in a suggestive location, stating 'Cynan was here'. It should be noted that Cynan was one of Wales' most popular poets, and in one of his poems he had written about what he hoped to do when he was old and respectable. The three libellous words in the picture implied that Cynan was a womaniser, and therefore not respectable. He insisted that the publishers remove the picture and all references to him, and he also demanded that compensation be paid to him, which he would donate to a charity of his choice. While lawyers were discussing the case, *Lol* was still being sold, with the offending picture included, through the back flap of the publishers' tent on the Eisteddfod field. Eventually, the publishers were ordered to pay a £50 fine and told to remove the picture and the implied reference to Cynan's dalliance with 'Shan'. In addition to the hundreds of uncensored copies which had already been sold, a box displaying the words 'Cynan's Charity Fund' had been placed at the front of the tent, and was overflowing with money donated by supporters of the publishers and *Lol*, which sold far more copies than it would have had the censor not censored the magazine.

Meanwhile, back in the White Lion, Lyn Ebenezer, a journalist and keen eisteddfodwr, had taken a friend to look for author Caradog Pritchard and his family, including Benji, the performing dog who had joined Ryan on stage in a previous chapter! Unfortunately for Lyn and his friend, Caradog had retired for an early night, but Mattie insisted on going upstairs to rouse him from his slumbers, and indeed, after a short while, he appeared, dressed in his pyjamas and smoking a cigarette. Mattie dressed him in a pacamac, stuck a pair of shoes on his feet and led him, his admirers and Benji in the direction of the Green, where Tawe Griffith was still conducting the singing.

On the first morning of the Eisteddfod, the president for the day was introduced to the audience. He was the local MP William Edwards, who had succeeded in persuading the military authorities in RAF Valley on Anglesey not to fly their jets over the Eisteddfod field during the week. A grateful audience stood and applauded him while he walked up the steps to the stage to give his presidential address. Unfortunately, the opening words of the speech of the local hero, who had apparently succeeded in stopping the jets, were drowned out by the roar of a jet flying over the pavilion and the field. I, for one, would dearly like to know what Wil Edwards muttered to himself while waiting for the sound of the jet to fade away.

During the week, the nascent Cwmni Theatr Cymru (Welsh Theatre Company) was performing *Cymru Fydd* ('Tomorrow's Wales'), a commissioned play by Saunders Lewis. The company would be formally established the following year by Wilbert Lloyd Roberts and go on to great success over the following decades. The production in Bala was given a warm welcome – perhaps too much so. The curtains at the back of the stage had started smouldering before the performance began. Lisabeth Miles and John Ogwen were the two unsuspecting actors on stage when the curtains eventually went up in flames behind them. John recalls the audience's reaction:

> At the beginning of the second act, I could see that the audience was restless, and I remember thinking, 'Surely we're not that bad, are we?' Then I smelled smoke, and somebody shouted 'Fire!'

But no-one panicked. No-one rushed for the doors. Elfyn Pritchard was there, and he recalls two things that happened which had a calming effect on the situation. First, instead of leaving the stage, John and Lisabeth sat quietly on a sofa on the set, and secondly, a member of the audience stood up and asked everyone to sit down, which they did. Eventually, the audience left the hall in an orderly fashion. On the way out, one of the actors was heard to say, '*Sinders* Lewis, my eye. It's a pity that his play didn't set the audience on fire!'

The Welsh Theatre Company was also responsible for a satirical evening called 'That's what we think', based on *Stiwdio B*, in which Ronnie starred, and strongly influenced by *That Was the Week That Was*. One of the actors, Gaynor Morgan Rees, remembers that in one episode, she and Mari Griffith, a popular folk singer at the time, wore tall black hats and black leotards 'which showed our legs'. The BBC received complaints from viewers who felt that the leggy display showed a lack of respect towards the Welsh national costume. Quite right! For shame! The BBC did consider taking the series off air, but the programme gained in popularity, and the storm abated.

As for the satirical evening at the Eisteddfod, it was all about aiming a kick squarely at the establishment's backside. The irreverent production poked fun at everything and everyone in Wales, including the National Eisteddfod itself. But perhaps most significantly, it was also the first time that Ryan and Ronnie performed together in public. The audience showed their appreciation with thunderous applause. Ryan and Ronnie had begun their journey towards enormous popularity and a place in the nation's hearts.

Ryan and Ronnie –
the early performances

Although the combination of Ryan and Ronnie was born on the stage of the National Eisteddfod in 1967, the act had been conceived months before by Meredydd Evans. He had already created a wide range of programmes which included quizzes, music programmes, comedy programmes with Ryan and *Stiwdio B*. But he was still looking for a comedy duo in the tradition of Abbot and Costello, Mike and Bernie Winters and especially Morecambe and Wise. They had their own television show, *Two of a Kind*, on ATV in 1967 before they moved over to the BBC in 1968 and appeared in *The Morecambe and Wise Show* until 1977. Merêd knew that Ronnie and Ryan worked well individually, and he needed to be convinced that they could work together as a double act, with Ronnie as the straight man. So a comedy and music pilot programme was produced specifically to test their compatibility.

According to Mari Griffith, who was in the review at the 1967 Eisteddfod, 'Ryan and Ronnie was an arranged marriage, brokered by Merêd, who had also decided on the order of service.' Ryan and Ronnie took part with Johnny Tudor and Gillian Thomas. Johnny Tudor was already a seasoned song and dance man, with the added experience of having worked the nightclubs outside Wales. Gillian Thomas was the lead singer of Y Triban, a very popular folk group in Wales at the time. The pilot worked, and the series *Ryan a Ronnie, Gill a Johnny* was commissioned. Thirty years later, sitting on a hill overlooking the town of Cardigan, Ronnie talked about those early beginings on a TV current affairs programme:

> Meredydd Evans had this idea of putting me and Ryan together. I didn't want it. I said no, I was quite happy as I was. Merêd lost his temper. He started shouting and swearing and banging the desk. I said, 'OK, OK. Anything for a quiet life.'

Accepting Ronnie's version of events is quite difficult in view of the comedy duo's enormous success as a result of Merêd's decision. It has to be remembered that Ronnie's words were spoken by a man who by this time had become an embittered alcoholic. He felt that he had never received the recognition he deserved and, sadly, always blamed everyone except himself for his own predicament.

But let's wind the clock back and join the audience in the small television studio for a recording of one of the first *Ryan and Ronnie* programmes. 'Stand by.' It's the voice of the floor manager counting down the final ten seconds. 'Cue the music ... Cue Ronnie ...' As the opening music fades, Ronnie enters through the applauding audience with a big smile on his face. He's dressed in a wine-coloured, high-collared velvet suit with the fashionable flared trousers of the 1960s. His bow tie matches his suit, and complements his pink shirt. 'Good evening, ladies and gentlemen. Welcome to another episode of *Ryan and Ronnie*. Tonight ...'

His opening remarks are interrupted by singing in the distance. Eventually, Ryan appears. He is wearing a pair of long shorts, a brightly-coloured Hawaiian shirt, a straw hat and sunglasses. His left arm is squeezing a big yellow plastic duck and under his right arm is a deckchair. Not a word has been spoken, and yet the audience is in stitches. Ryan stares at Ronnie. Ronnie stares at Ryan, and although they've rehearsed this routine many times, Ronnie's finding it very difficult not to laugh. But he daren't. After all, he is the straight man. His job is to feed Ryan the lines that will get him the laughs. Let's freeze the frame for a moment. Every famous comedian has certain facial attributes that makes that person memorable. Ken Dodd has his teeth and hair, Les Dawson, his tired face, Tommy Cooper, his large head and manic laugh. With Ryan, it was the nose, which almost touched his chin, making him look like Punch in profile. He had a small body and was quicksilver on his feet, never still, always darting around like a Tasmanian devil or one of those pink rabbits whose batteries never run out. He had energy to spare. Ryan was the little brother, intent on creating havoc, and Ronnie tried his best to keep him in check. Meanwhile, in our freeze-frame, Ronnie's still staring motionlessly at Ryan, and the look on his face suggests that he believes his partner, as they say in Carmarthen, 'is completely off his head'. Ronnie's waiting for the laughter to subside, and when it does, he asks Ryan:

Ronnie: Where have *you* been?

Ryan: Blackpool. Blackpool, Ron, on my holidays. You see, I missed the summer last year.

Ronnie: How?

Ryan: I was in the bath at the time. And do you know what, Ron?

Ronnie: What, Ry?

Ryan: I was ill. Very ill.

Ronnie: Were you?

Ryan: Yes, mun. I've just told you I was.

Ronnie: What was the matter?

Ryan: I ate a rabbit in the bed and breakfast I was staying in. And I had a bad stomach.

Ronnie: A bad stomach?

Ryan: You're absolutely right, Ron, and myxomatosis.

Ronnie: Did you go to the doctor's?

Ryan: Yes. And do you know what he gave me?

Ronnie: Castor oil to pour down your throat?

Ryan: No. A ferret to stick down my trousers.

Vintage Ryan and Ronnie. The audience is lapping it up when, without warning, Ryan, obviously improvising, targets one of them.

That's right, Mrs Jones. You have a good laugh. It's good for you. Go on, show your teeth. No! No! Don't take 'em out, woman. What's wrong with you?

More laughter. It's time for Ronnie to step in.

Ronnie: RYAN!

Ryan: Ron. I've been meaning to tell you …

Ronnie: Tell me what?

Ryan: I'm going on holiday before long, to Spain.

Ronnie: Where in Spain?

Ryan: Maj-orca.

Ronnie: No, Ry. Its not Maj-orca. That's not how you say it. You're suppose to say Mai-orca. Its not a 'j', it's an 'i'.

Ryan: Mai-orca. Not Maj-orca. Mai-orca.

Ronnie: That's it. Mai-orca.

Ryan: Mai-orca.

Ronnie: That's it. Perfect. Mai-orca! When are you going?

Ryan: End of Iune, beginning of Iuly.

During the applause, a film is shown. Ryan and Ronnie are dressed as Indians, carrying a long carpet. They are both scantily dressed, wearing turbans, and trying unsuccefully to cross a very busy road. Eventually, Ryan has an idea. They unroll the carpet. It is in fact a portable zebra crossing. The cars screech to a halt and they cross safely, acknowledging the irate car drivers with a smile. We then move on to the next sketch – one of my favourites.

The opening wide-angle shot shows a long, winding, narrow road in the Rhondda, disappearing from view. A white Jaguar car comes into shot with the words 'White Tide Washing Powder' written on the door. Out of the car steps Ronnie. He is the White Tide man. And to press home the point, he is dressed from head to toe in white: top hat, shirt and bow tie, jacket and trousers and shoes. His white-gloved hand is clutching a bundle of pound notes, which he waves at the camera, saying, 'I'm the White Tide man. If you recognise me, there's five pounds in it for you.' He walks away from the camera down a narrow path to the front door of a house. We follow him. He knocks. A small, wizened old lady with a shawl over her shoulders appears in the doorway. It's Ryan. She looks at the strange apparition dressed in white as if he's landed on the doorstep from another planet, and in a small, squeaky voice, manages to utter a one-word question: 'Yes?' What she really means is: 'What the hell are you doing on my doorstep dressed in that ridiculous outfit, and what do you want?' Ronnie holds the money under her nose. 'Madam. If you can tell me who I am, there's five pounds in it for you.' Ryan looks at Ronnie in disbelief, cocks his head to one side, moves ever so slightly towards Ronnie, who towers above him, looks him up and down and inquires, 'Are you Gladys's boy?'

They would use the same location for a filmed insert in a later programme, where Ryan, dressed as the 'Valleys Mam', is talking over the wall to her next-door neighbour.

Ryan: I hear your Gladys is getting married on Saturday.

Ronnie: Yes.

Ryan: Pregnant is she?

Ronnie: No.

Ryan: Oh! There's posh!

Meanwhile, back in the studio, Ronnie introduces the Richard Williams Singers, with Ryan as the soloist. He's been rehearsing with the singers and the director during the afternoon, but now he's nowhere to be seen, and the choir has started singing. What happens next is a complete surprise to the audience and the conductor. Having sung a few 'Kalin-ka, Kalin-ka, Kalin-kas', suddenly, on the last 'ka', Ryan jumps into view from the middle of the choir, dressed as a Cossack. He's wearing an oversized fur hat, and a pair of spectacles that look as if he's borrowed them from Trotsky. He holds the 'ka' note for ages, walking towards conductor Richard Williams and stopping within a millimetre of his nose, still singing. This Russian attack is designed to unnerve the conductor and make him laugh, which it does. None of this apparent improvisation has happened in rehearsal. Only the director and Ryan know what will happen next. He is hell-bent on making it as difficult as possible for the choir to carry on as he crouches into the Cossack kick position. Dancing and singing at the same time, his bravura performance finally ends with Ryan jumping in the air and letting out a yell of satisfaction, to thunderous applause from the audience. If I had to choose a performance which encapsulates Ryan's diverse talents, this would be it.

Ryan was the personification of versatility. He was an actor who could sing, a singer who could mime and move gracefully, a consummate performer who could make you laugh with a sly look and a well-timed 'Jiw, jiw'. Over the course of Ryan and Ronnie's five-year partnership, Ryan was doing more singing, acting, and presenting on other programmes in Welsh and English, preparing the ground for that time in the future when he and Ronnie might no longer be a comedy double act. Ronnie, on the other hand, was quite happy in the moment, living for the present, without preparing in any way for the future. As Ryan's straight man, Ronnie was able to observe his partner's versatility at close quarters, and it's true to say that, in the early days at least, Ronnie was one of Ryan's biggest admirers. In his own words:

> Ryan was the funniest person I have ever met. He had a big heart and an unbelievable sense of timing. When you're working together in a double act, timing is everything. It can't be learned. You're born with it, or you're not.

In spite of the praise lavished on Ryan by Ronnie and others, it should be remembered that all their comedy material was written by Ronnie and, as Alfred Hitchcock put it, the three most important parts of a film are 'the script, and the script and the script.' Ryan needed Ronnie's words in order to bring his characters to life. They would always work together on creating new characters, though – Phyllis the barmaid, for instance. How would she look? What would she wear? Would she have a Valleys accent, or was she from Swansea? Ryan became Phyllis once he donned the beehive hairdo, the thick black mascara and bright pink lipstick, standing behind the bar, arms folded, looking for all the world like an elderly Barbie doll. Then, Ronnie's words breathed life into Phyllis, and completed Ryan's memorable characterisation:

> Well, jiw, jiw. 'Ow are you, then? You alright, cariad? Out with your 'usband, are you, or are you with somebody you like for a change? ... Oh, look! There's a woman over there with a very low-cut dress, jiw jiw, showing everything ... Oh, sorry, no, I'm wrong – it's two bald men sitting next to each other ...

Ronnie explained how they worked together when he was interviewed before their first television series:

> I wrote all the shows, and usually left it till the last minute. I remember meeting Galton and Simpson, who wrote *Steptoe and Son*. They'd been given a year to write the series, but they actually wrote it in the last three weeks. I always wrote in bed, with my wife reminding me every five minutes that the script had to be in by lunchtime that day. And somehow or other, when the adrenalin started pumping, it was. Ryan wrote all the songs, and he was the centre of attention. But when the audience laughed at Ryan's jokes, it gave me great satisfaction too, because I knew they were laughing at my material. The fact that Ryan received more attention than me didn't bother me. Of course we would disagree, but after a pint, it was all forgotten.

Over the years, however, Ronnie became bitter, resentful and jealous of Ryan's star status. Everybody wanted his autograph, and they would bypass Ronnie to get it. That's why the title of

Meic Povey's play about the two comedians is so telling: *The Life of Ryan ... and Ronnie*. The ellipse emphasised the growing gulf in their relationship, and the relegation of Ronnie to the role of straight man, an afterthought in the eyes of the public. Carl Jung said, 'the brighter the light, the blacker the shadow'. Ryan always stood centre stage, in the spotlight, and that light blinded people to Ronnie's presence. Dazzled by Ryan's brilliance, they were unable to see how important, indeed, how essential was Ronnie's contribution to the partnership. Ronnie always walked in Ryan's shadow. And when the bright light of Ryan's talents was extinguished by his untimely death in 1977, Ronnie ceased to exist as well until he reappeared almost fifteen years later in a popular comedy series on S4C called *Licyris Olsorts* ('Liquorice Allsorts'). But as we shall see, although his life became a constant fight against depression, alcoholism and the feeling of rejection, those intervening years after Ryan's death were, at times, very productive.

After creating a huge following for their television series, the next step was to leave the confines of the studio and tour Wales, giving the fans an opportunity to meet their heroes. The main compère on stage was usually Alun Williams, a very popular broadcaster on television and radio, and an energetic accompanist. Margaret Williams and Bryn Williams were the soloists in the early days. If Alun happened to be away, Glan Davies or I would step into the breach. It seemed that every secretary of every village hall and club in Wales wanted Ryan and Ronnie to appear on their stage. So it was decided to form a production company to deal with the increasing demand, and on our first tour we visited halls in Haverfordwest, Aberystwyth, Bala, Pwllheli, Porthaethwy and Llanidloes. The company even ventured into the world of disco dancing, a new phenomenon at the time. This presented a slight problem for two reasons. First, there weren't any records being produced at the time in the Welsh language which you could dance to. Secondly, no village hall in Wales had decks on which to play any kind of record. Presented with a similar survival problem due to some local flooding, Noah built an ark. We built a discotheque. Two decks to play 45s and LPs, with lights pulsating to the beat of the music, were placed in a purpose-built desk, which was decorated with the best copper panels the local ironmongers could supply, artistically stuck on with glue. Very tasteful! Ronnie and I shared a disco for four nights at the Halfway pub in Nantgaredig during the 1970 Eisteddfod in Ammanford, alternating Welsh songs with instrumentals by Booker T. and the M.G.'s, B. Bumble and the Stingers, and Percy Faith and his Orchestra, who provided 'smooching' music with the theme from the film *A Summer Place*. One evening, some members of the Welsh Language Society paid me a visit, and held a pint of beer in a threatening manner over the decks, warning me that unless I stopped playing the instrumental music, then the Terminator would return and pour the contents of the glass all over the kit. So that evening, Booker T. and B. Bumble took the night off!

The company that was formed to look after Ryan and Ronnie was called the Wales Production Company, and the emphasis on 'production' meant that Ryan and Ronnie swept the stage clean of amateurism, and brought professionalism to the events and venues at which they appeared. It was a stage version of their television show, with lights, microphones, make-up, smart suits, posh frocks, a band, a running order and a rehearsal. Some of Wales' most popular performers would be part of the show, including Cardiff group the Hennessys, Heather Jones, Margaret Williams, Bryn Williams, Triban and Tony and Aloma. Everyone came. If the show started at 7.30, the performers were expected to be there for a soundcheck at 5.30. At 7.20, the compère would be standing in the wings with the first act standing behind him. At 7.29, the light in the hall would be dimmed, a spotlight would fall on the curtains, and an out of vision voice would announce, 'Ladies and gentlemen, welcome to the show. Your host this evening is Alun Williams.'

On the dot at 7.30, the curtains would open, the band would strike up and Alun would walk out to the centre of the stage, immaculately dressed in a dinner suit with a black bow tie, starting the evening in style. Of course, things didn't always run that smoothly. I remember going with Ryan and Ronnie to Rhosllanerchrugog – the largest village in Wales, as the inhabitants always like to remind you. We were playing the Institute, which I'm sure holds more people than Carnegie Hall, and which had been full the previous evening for a production by the Welsh Theatre Company. At 7.30, out I went on stage, to face an almost empty hall. There were fifty people in an auditorium which could hold 2,000. Undaunted, I launched into my warm-up act:

Good evening, ladies and gentlemen. May I say most sincerely what a privilege and pleasure it is for you to have me here tonight. [Pause for guaranteed laugh from the audience. Nothing!] Before I go any further, the management would like me to ask you can you please move. We want the pretty ladies in the front, and the ... Oh! I see you've moved back already. [Pause for another guaranteed laugh. Nothing.]

The previous night in Llanidloes, the audience had enjoyed being poked fun at by the cheeky young presenter. And wasn't it the great Bob Monkhouse who said, 'Why should I change my material when the audience changes?' But Bob Monkhouse had never played to an almost empty house in Rhos. As I stood there, I felt that the auditorium had doubled in size and the audience had halved in number. My job was to warm up the audience, but the atmosphere was as cold as a graveyard under two feet of snow. And things were about to get worse, as I attempted a personal appeal, indeed a cry for help, to one member of the audience in particular. The one man who could save me, perhaps, from dying on the stage of the Institute. I continued:

> Everytime I come to Rhos to interview people for the BBC, I always make sure that I speak to Mr Ivor Green. It doesn't matter how busy he is, he's always ready to answer a few questions, and always prepared to give me his honest opinion on the day's news. He's also very supportive of any production that comes here to his beloved Rhos. So, Mr Ivor Green, are you here tonight?

I waited hopefully to hear his voice, but instead, someone shouted out, 'He died a fortnight ago.' This interjection was like a bullet shot at me from the darkness. In my panic, I was tempted to say, 'Well. For everybody except Ivor Green then, here are ... Ryan and Ronnie.' But my thoughts were interrupted by a panicky whisper from the wings: 'Keep going! Ryan's been caught in traffic.' So I kept going, filling five minutes with one of Ryan's jokes about an articulated lorry carrying cars. Travelling along the road, the driver suddenly loses his headlights. He decides to climb up to the top deck of cars and switch on the lights of the car at the front. Problem solved. The beam lit up the whole countryside. Driving around a corner, the driver could hear the screeching of brakes in the far distance, and eventually he saw a car in the ditch and a frightened little man standing next to it. The lorry driver asked him, 'Why is your car in the ditch? Couldn't you see my lights?' To which the quivering driver replied, 'Yes! I could see your lights miles away, and I thought to myself, if it's that high, how wide is it going to be?'

From what I remember, there was an audible titter from the audience, and a thumbs up from the wings to let me know that Ryan and Ronnie had arrived. After a quick introduction, onstage they came. They sang 'Delilah', and then Ryan apologised for being late, explaining that a broken-down lorry was to blame. Unfortunately, he then added: 'Which reminds me of a story about a lorry driver carrying cars on an articulated lorry, when something happened to his headlights …'

NO! NO! He was about to repeat the joke I had just stolen from him. TOO LATE! The joke, which was usually met with laughter and thunderous applause when Ryan told it, was greeted by a stunned silence from the audience, and the boys quickly moved on to a song. During the interval, having been told what I had done, Ryan let me know what he thought of me in no uncertain terms. I had learned an important lesson, and in fact I learned a great deal about performing in front of a live audience from both of them when we were on the road. They were some of the happiest days of my life as a broadcaster and presenter.

London and Blackpool

' At last, a new comedy show to enthuse about. Sandwiched between *The Clangers* and *Marine Boy* at the unlikely time of 4.55, BBC Wales have come up with their own bright, mini-*Rowan & Martin's Laugh-in* [an American comedy series] which, if not particularly original, is a concept which was presented with much style and professionalism,' according to the *Radio Times* of the day.

Bill Cotton, the head of light entertainment at the BBC in London, had taken a chance on Ryan and Ronnie, having seen the recording of a programme they had done in English which was broadcast on St. David's Day 1970. Three series were made for the English network between 1971 and 1973 but, unfortunately, they didn't go down well. Ryan and Ronnie weren't happy either, and admitted to Mark Lewisham, who was writing about comedy on television, that they did not feel as comfortable working in English as they did in Welsh. The BBC's audience research seemed to bear that out, as these comments show:

Jokes and sketches were corny, and although they worked hard enough they failed to click.

Although Ryan Davies and Ronnie Williams are talented enough, they need much better material if they're to make it to the top.

The funniest part of the show is the sketch about the dysfunctional family.

This last referred to 'Our House', which Ronnie had written while he was still at Cwm Gwendraeth Grammar School all those years ago, and it became a firm favourite with the show's audience, with the instantly recognisable punchline, 'Don't call Will on your father!'

By the second series, the team of writers had increasd to twelve, but the standard of the comedy declined with every programme. It was felt that it was village hall stuff that might pass muster on a 'local' network (meaning Wales), but was not up to the standard required to be shown throughout the UK, and not a good advert for Welsh variety, either. The BBC's Shaun Sutton, head of drama in London at the time, thought it impossible that they could be any less funny than they had been in the previous series. But they were. Even Owen Edwards, head of programmes for the BBC in Wales, had to agree that the material was very weak, and that Ryan and Ronnie were not at their best in English. And yet, despite the criticism on all sides, they both felt confident enough to accept an offer to appear in a show called *Those Were the Days* on the pier in Blackpool. According to Einir, Ronnie's first wife, those were the very days when Ronnie began to feel very unhappy. In his words:

> We were expected to lose our Welsh identity and become northern comics when we went to Blackpool. So there wasn't much point going there. We didn't want people to laugh at us because we were Welsh, but because we were funny. And the two things seemed to be inseperable.

According to Einir:

> Working non-stop had an adverse effect on his health, resulting in bouts of depression which caused him to

turn nasty and mistreat me physically. He very rarely came home to see me or the children, and if he wasn't in Blackpool or in the studio, he was on the road. He had plenty of opportunities to have his flings.

While Ryan and Ronnie were appearing in *Those were the Days*, they were also preparing for their next Welsh TV series, which would be recorded when their Blackpool season came to an end. And to add to their already punishing schedule, Ryan was also working on a solo project with Richard Burton, filming Dylan Thomas' *Under Milk Wood* in Fishguard.

There were occasions when Einir and Irene and their children went to see Ryan and Ronnie in Blackpool, but the two familes never stayed together. Ronnie began an affair with Lavinia, one of the dancers in the show, which eventually led to Einir and Ronnie's divorce. While I was writing this book, I discovered that Lavinia is now keeping a pub in Cardiff, and went to talk to her. It was obvious from her reminiscences about the Blackpool days that she felt that the relationship between Ryan and Ronnie was not a happy one. She saw Ryan as the confident one, while Ronnie was depressed. Ryan enjoyed the singing and the dancing; Ronnie worried about having to do either. It's true to say that Ryan missed his family and, according to Irene, it was during this time that he composed one of his best, and best-known songs, 'Pan fo'r Nos yn Hir' ('When the night is long'), in which he expresses his feeling of loneliness at night, with the dawn seemingly so far away. He wrote a letter from Blackpool to his Uncle Brinley, the former Archdruid, which suggests that he was happier when members of the family were around him.

Central Pier

Blackpool

Dear Archdruid and Mrs. Arch [his Auntie Muriel]
Greetings from the lands of the North. As you can see,
I'm in Blackpool, trying to entertain the natives. Mam,
Anti Sap and Uncle Ernie have been here for a week,
looking after me, stuffing me with food and so on. The
family will be up in a fortnight. Of course, I go down
every Saturday and spend Sunday with them.

Unlike Ronnie, Ryan had boundless stamina and enthusiasm
and, in spite of the criticism, he was still keen to gain more
experience by appearing on television in English, thereby
appealing to a wider audience. Ronnie was happier performing
on his home patch in Wales. Ryan's horizons were wider. He
could see himself in the future, entertaining audiences outside
Wales and England, not purely as a singer, or a comedian, or a
musician or a dancer, but as an all-round entertainer, combining
all his talents. In fact, like his hero, Sammy Davis, Jr., Ryan
admitted as much in an interview for *The Times*, when he
was asked by Trevor Fishlock if he would like to work in
England.

Of course I want British recognition. Like all performers,
I have my ego as well, and I want to get the show on
the road. But Wales is my home, and I want to help to
develop Welsh entertainment. I would hate to hear people
saying that Ryan Davies has sold out to the English, and
turned his back on his own people. The problem is, how
do I realise my ambitions without compromising my
principles?

As we shall see later on, by 1972 discussions were already under way with the BBC in London to develop Ryan as a performer on English television. Ronnie was not included in these discussions. In July, another show in the *Ryan and Ronnie* series was aired in Wales, and such was the following they had in south Wales in both languages that the Grand Theatre in Swansea invited them to appear in their Christmas pantomime, *Cinderella*. They filled the Grand for three months, and the run had to be extended. Furthermore, they were booked immediately for the following year's pantomime, *Dick Whittington* (ironically, about a young man who wanted to go to London because he'd heard that the streets were paved with gold).

The newspapers were full of praise. 'It seems certain that this comedy partnership will enjoy many more years at the Grand,' said one. But it was not to be. Six months later, when they were playing at the Double Diamond Club in Caerphilly, Tommy Cooper's home town, they were in the headlines once again, but this time for all the wrong reasons: 'Ryan and Ron to split!', 'The thin one goes it alone!', 'Ryan and Ronnie bow out'.

Ronnie had reached the end of the line. Televison in Welsh and English, a summer season in Blackpool, concerts on the road, excessive drinking and personal problems all took their toll on him:

> The more successful you are, the more difficult it is to maintain the high standards you've set for yourself. I didn't want to split up the partnership, but I was ill at the time through working too hard.

In his play *The Life of Ryan ... and Ronnie*, Meic Povey suggests, quite rightly, that Ronnie would have been happy as a famous personality in Wales, enjoying 'the well-lubricated hospitality of the fans', as one newspaper put it. Unlike Ryan, he didn't yearn for a wider audience, as Bill Cotton found out when he made Ryan and Ronnie an offer which flew in the face of all the criticism levelled at their English television series. 'Thank you, boys, for three great series. Now it's the big time. You'll get your own 50-minute slot, and international guests.' Ronnie didn't feel he could deal with such an offer.

I was working all the time, and nothing meant anything any more, not even Bill Cotton's praise. We got the offer in January, and I became ill in May. I suppose I had enjoyed the first two years of working in Welsh, and even the first year in English. But we had to do more and more all the time. A summer season for four months a year, performing two shows a night. We worked the northern clubs, although we weren't comfortable working in English. Life had been reduced to a vicious circle of sleeping and working. There was no reason to live. I don't remember seeing my children growing up. I was never there. I started drinking heavily – two or three pints before the show, and more after the recording. I didn't tell Ryan how I was feeling. I couldn't discuss personal problems with him. So I went to see a psychiatrist friend, hoping he'd give me some tablets or something, but he said that I had to stop performing immediately because I was heading for a mental breakdown. I told him I couldn't possibly stop in the middle of a week in the Double Diamond. Anyway, I went back to the club, and Ryan was in the dressing room. Without turning around, he asked me what was wrong, and I told him that I had to stop. He grabbed me in a hug, and we both cried. He offered to go on stage by himself, but I said no.

The psychiatrist Ronnie referred to was the late Dafydd Huws, who told me more about what happened on the morning Ronnie went to see him.

Ronnie was very tired, and in a depressed state. He needed a long break to recover his health and overall strength. But I felt that something else was worrying him, and that this was the root cause of his problem. It was obvious to me that Ryan could carry on without Ronnie. He was receiving invitations to do his solo act, and that made Ronnie feel unwanted, lonely and frustrated. Ryan could be independent and work in both languages, and his success no longer depended on having Ronnie as his straight man. Ronnie knew that, and he also knew that it was going to be very difficult for him to face a future without Ryan.

Ryan's son, Arwyn, had this to say about the situation:

Whatever people said and wrote about the break-up, the truth was that they were good friends. Ronnie was a great straight man. It's very difficult to stand on stage watching someone else get all the laughs.

Against the psychiatrist's advice, Ronnie returned to the stage of the Double Diamond Club, and he and Ryan gave their final performance on 6 May 1974. In the *South Wales Echo*, Alex McKinty agreed with Dafydd Huws' assessment of the future for both Ryan and Ronnie:

With all due respect to Ronnie Williams, who was suffering from nervous exhaustion, I'd say that Ryan Davies now stands a better chance of making the major breakthrough that his natural talent deserves.

A mere five months after the break-up, Ryan had begun filming a solo television series in Pembrokeshire, and was back in the Double Diamond Club recording a cabaret show. In the meantime, Ronnie had turned his back on the television industry, preferring to escape to Cerrigydrudion with his family, and run a pub.

After the split
and *Under Milk Wood*

Although Ryan and Ronnie were often compared to Morecambe and Wise, a comparison with the Two Ronnies would have been more accurate, since they, like Barker and Corbett, worked on individual projects as well as the double act. Ryan quite often played the role of quizmaster, and in 1968 he played the main part in an early television play about the drummer of a local band who eventually stands up to his nagging wife. This was the first Welsh play on television to be shown with English subtitles. It was called, simply, *Y Drwmwr* ('The Drummer'). Pop concerts were gaining in popularity in Wales at the end of the 1960s due to an explosion in the Welsh-language pop scene. One of the most popular groups of the day was Hogia Llandegai from north Wales, who maintained in one of their songs that 'In Wales, everyone plays a guitar these days.' In 1968, they headlined the first Welsh-language pop festival in the west Wales village of Pontrhydfendigaid, where Ryan was the main presenter. Ryan was also busy presenting programmes for schools on radio and television, and working in the evenings doing his one-man cabaret show in clubs all over south Wales. His energy seemed boundless.

Ronnie was not as busy as Ryan, but he did produce a radio programme called *Pop Wales*, and present an evening chat show with Welsh personalities for BBC Wales. *Pop Wales* did what it said on the tin, discussing pop music in Wales with Welsh singers and groups. Shirley Bassey, Harry Secombe, Andy

Fairweather Low from Amen Corner and Tom Jones were some of the stars interviewed by the presenter Endaf Emlyn, himself a great pop singer/songwriter. Endaf remembers doing an interview with Tom Jones outside the Rank in Southampton while Gordon Mills, Tom's manager at the time, looked on. Tom had been talking about the travelling he was doing all over the world, and it was all going well until Endaf asked him, 'So, Tom, after doing all this travelling, where do you call home?' Tom answered, 'Sunbury-on-Thames.' Like a shot, Gordon Mills was heard to shout: 'Cut!' He had a word in Ronnie's ear, and then spoke to Tom. Ronnie spoke to Endaf. Although Tom had given the correct answer, Gordon Mills knew that the correct answer is not always the best one. Ronnie cued Endaf, who asked the question again. Looking as humble as he could, Tom replied, 'Well, it's true that I do travel quite a bit, but wherever I am, Ponty will always be home for me.' Of course it will, Tom – a much better answer than the green, green grass of Sunbury-on-Thames. Ronnie also presented a pop programme on television on Saturdays, and one young girl who remembers coming down to Cardiff to sing on the programme told me that Ronnie was a very suave-looking man, especially when he wore his turtleneck sweater and blazer. She and other members of her group remember being taken to the BBC Club by Ronnie after the show, and it was obvious that he enjoyed talking about the BBC, and that he was very proud of the corporation.

In 1972, the director Andrew Sinclair was casting a film version of *Under Milk Wood*, and Ryan was given one of the main parts, alongside Richard Burton and Peter O'Toole. Sinclair tells the story of a visit he and Ryan made to London to meet Burton in order to try and persuade Elizabeth Talyor to play the part of Rosie Probert. Burton was kicking his heels in London for three months while Taylor was filming *Zee and Co*. The discussion became a drinking session, with Sinclair and Ryan drinking out of silver tankards given 'To Elizabeth Taylor and Richard Burton, from the grateful people of Wales', according to the inscriptions on them. Under the influence of drink, Burton promised Sinclair that, out of respect to his friend Dylan Thomas, he would remain sober throughout the filming. Sinclair asked him what exactly he meant. 'It means,' said Burton, 'that I'll only drink two bottles of vodka a day instead of my usual four.'

Many hours, and more bottles later, Elizabeth Taylor arrived, unannounced, wearing a pair of yellow hot pants, according to Sinclair, and a mink coat. When she saw that Sinclair and Ryan were drinking out of the silver tankards, she flew into a rage. Burton then made the mistake of telling her that he had given the tankards to his now bosom friends, and the shouting from Miss Taylor's direction turned into uncontrollable, hysterical shrieking. It was then, according to Sinclair, that he and Ryan left, without the tankards, presumably.

According to the Welsh press at the time, this was the film which would bring Ryan international recognition as a performer, but it was not to be. In fact, the adaptation got a very tepid reception, in Wales at least. Sinclair had taken Dylan Thomas' simple story about the lives of the colourful characters of Llareggub and thrown some of his own weird and wonderful ideas into the mix until there was bugger all left of the original story. He saw images of Celtic mythology in the original work, and references to the living dead and the devil himself, played by Burton. He filmed some of the villagers dancing around the tavern, eventually dancing out to sea and turning into seals. And what of Ryan's and Burton's characters?

I had given the two Voices faces and characters, giving predominance to the powerful, brooding face and pale, piercing eyes of Richard Burton, foolery to the thin, playful, melancholic skull's head of Ryan Davies, the beloved clown of Welsh television, playing the jester to Burton's King; the imp to Lucifer.

One remark by Sinclair proves without doubt that he was lost within his own vision and interpretation of Dylan's work as a fable from the Middle Ages, with Celtic undertones:

I added one thing which ties up the film nicely. In medieval legend, the devil rides a pig, and we have the Second Voice, Ryan, jumping on a pig and riding straight into camera. It's a hell of a shot!

In fact, it was Ryan who suggested that he jump onto the pig's back and ride him, rodeo-style, until he was thrown off into the mud. *The Guardian*'s film critic was left in no doubt as to the merit of the film. It had none.

While the prospect of Eastman-coloured *Under Milk Wood* is guaranteed to wring hosannahs from the American Ladies' Literary Guild and sixth-formers in first beards, I must admit, it sounds to me like a sure basis for a sloe-black, slow, black, crow black, cockle-boat-bobbing nightmare.

Burton also had his doubts. 'Dylan wrote *Milk Wood* for radio, and I don't know if he would have liked this film at all,' he said. Ryan spoke up for Sinclair by saying that at least he had come to Wales to look for his cast, rather than using London actors. Be that as it may, the film was first shown, not in a cinema in Swansea, but in a festival in Vienna, with Italian subtitles.

While Ryan was filming *Under Milk Wood*, Ronnie was presenting a chat show on BBC Wales television, in English, called *Late Show*, and had gone down to Fishguard to speak to Ryan and Burton on set. Ronnie asks Burton first of all: 'What's it like to work with the great Ryan Davies?' Burton laughs, but is obviously embarrassed by the question, and Ryan shifts about uncomfortably in his chair. Watching this archive footage, I can't help feeling that Ronnie is slightly envious of the fact that he's the one asking the questions, and that Ryan is the one sitting next to Burton, getting all the attention. At the end of the interview, Ronnie turns to camera and fires one critical bullet in the direction of the production:

The film's budget is only a quarter of a million pounds, and with such a small budget, some form of financial success is assured. Artistic success may prove to be a little more elusive.

It could be argued that Ronnie's final remarks were mean-spirited, but the truth of the matter is that he was proved right. The film was a failure, and the only international recognition Ryan had was from the members of the audience who watched the film's premiere in Vienna.

While filming *Under Milk Wood*, Ryan was at the same time involved in the filming of the next *Ryan and Ronnie* series. He wrote to Richard Burton, who was in Italy at the time, to invite him to be a special guest on one of the shows. Burton's letter of reply is published here, in its entirety, for the first time.

Ryan as a young boy

Ryan, Irene, and Dai Bach, an old friend and neighbour, at the Llangollen Eisteddfod, 1955

Ryan and Irene on the Berwyn mountain range, 1959

At home in Llanfyllin: Don Roberts, W.T. Davies (Ryan's father), Irene, Nans (Ryan's mother and Ryan, 1959

The London Welsh Folk Dance party competing at the Llangollen Eisteddfod in the 1960s

A star-struck Ryan with friends at a London Welsh dinner, listening to Sir Geraint Evans

Ryan sporting a bow tie next to his best friend, Rhydderch Jones, at a birthday party in London

The London Welsh competing at an eisteddfod. On Ryan's right in the front is Howard Goodfellow, who won the duet competition with Ryan

Ryan as a surprised Charley's Aunt

Ryan and Irene in 1966

A very tall Irene!

Little Bethan with Ryan, his mother Nans and Irene, at Ryan's cousin Mair Davies' wedding

A cwtsh for Bethan and Dad

Arwyn being squashed by Dad

Ryan and the children in Dyffryn Gardens

A proud father

The quicksilver Ryan from Glanaman

The multi-talented Mr Davies

'Never B sharp, never B flat,
always B natural.'

"Arping on as always.'

Breaking a leg with Myfanwy Talog

Acting alongside Bill Owen in *The Sunshine Boys* at the New Theatre, Cardiff

Ryan Ponsonby Davies, Lord of the Manor, don't you know!

The dogged entertainer

Ryan with actress Gaynor Morgan Rees

Ephraim and Twm Twm: Guto Roberts and Ryan in the situation comedy *Fo a Fe*

Ryan, and a full house of children in the Grand Theatre, Swansea

David Lyn and a very surprised vicar

Ryan and Irene with Richard and Gwyneth Llywelyn at a party in Pontarddulais

The family on a cruise to the Canary Islands

A cartoon of Ryan by the *Western Mail* cartoonist Gren

A pencil sketch of Ryan by Clive Dunn, who took over from Ryan in the Grand Theare pantomime from 1977 onwards

Ryan and family sitting under the Lincoln Memorial in Washington DC

A family picnic in the Blue
Ridge Mountains of Virginia

Niagara. This was the last picture
ever taken of Ryan, standing with
Peter, the son of the family he was
staying with in America

The bronze bust of Ryan in the foyer of the BBC. The words are Ryan's: Laughter is the same in both languages

10 March 1973

Miramonti Majestic Grand Hotel
Cortina D'Amprezzo
Dolomiti, Italy

Thank you very much for the letter and your offer. I have just finished listening, on a powerful, short-wave radio, to the hysteria of our match against Ireland. Elizabeth, knowing my atavistic feelings on the subject of rugby, removed herself to the bedroom with an aspirin and a glass of white wine, praying to God that Wales would win. There was nobody to say it to, so she compromised by snarling at the walls of our suite, 'Wales must win. Wales must win. Otherwise, I have a husband sodden with melancholia for a week. Also, if Wales win, I might get a present.'

Well done. We won. So I will have to buy her a present. Let us pretend that I am not shivering at the closeness of the match, and answer your letter.

I would be delighted to be on your programme, but she wants to be on it too, and we couldn't possibly set foot in the UK for at least another twelve months or so. Can you persuade the money boys of the Be Be Eck [the phonetic pronounciation of BBC in Welsh] to come together with Ronnie and yourself to wherever we are at the time? We are almost certain to be in Rome, or possibly Spain. Normally, I would not appear on the BBC as we are heavy shareholders in Harlech Television, but for you, we are prepared to be relatively dichotomous.

If the programme is to be in English about things Welsh, then it would be interesting, but not important, i.e., the BBC couldn't sell it anywhere outside Wales. Next: you couldn't possibly outrage us with an invitation to appear on a TV show with you. Both she and I consider you to be a man of extraordinary talent and vitality. Did you ever get the photostatted copies of the Amercan reviews of *Milk Wood*? They are sensational for you and me, and running us close were those for Elizabeth and the dreaded O'Toole. Of course, Shanco Thomas [Dylan] came off best of the lot. What an extraordinary thing it is, Ryan, that a prophet is without honour in his own country. To this day, as far as I know, Dylan has never been praised and lauded in Wales as he has been, albeit with some dissident voices, in every other country. The most vicious attackers of Tom Jones, the pop singer, are invariably Welsh. I have had a great many notices for *Under Milk Wood* in many languages, and with the help of a dictionary in Russian, Dutch and Swedish. They are almost paeans of praise for the film.

The pathetic little Welsh press damned the whole enterprise with the faintest of feeble praise. And when I think that I gave a thousand pounds to *Y Cymro* [the Welsh-language weekly newspaper] to keep it [going]. Ma fe'n ddigon i ala ti yn benwan [Burton adds in brackets, 'Pontrhydyfen *patois*'. It is, in fact, colloquial Welsh, and correct: 'It's enough to drive you mad.'] So, anyway, ysgrifennwch rhywbeth abythdi'r programme a phwy ['Write something about the programme and who's taking part.' He then adds, in English, that his mutations and Welsh syntax have been blown to smithereens.] Mae fy mutations, a fy syntax yn Gymraeg wedi mynd yn yfflon racs. A pwy yw'r bachan *in control*? ['Who's in charge?'] Rwy'n sicr y bydd y *producer* yn cael hwyl mwynhad iawn os bydd yn bosib i ni siarad am tymyd bach abythdi'r ffilm. ['I'm sure the producer will be very pleased if we can talk a little bit about the film.'] If you can spare the cash, send me the latest Geiriadur Newydd [Welsh dictionary]. I'll pay you back in hard liquor.

Yn dragwydd, Richard a'i wraig [Eternally yours, Richard and his wife]

One of the questions most often asked in Wales about Richard Burton is, 'How much Welsh did he speak?' I asked Graham, his brother, the same question, and the answer I got was tongue in cheek, I'm sure: 'Put it like this – the more vodka that went in, the more Welsh came out.'

One of Ryan's greatest admirers during the early 1970s was the deputy head of programmes at the BBC, Geraint Stanley Jones. He had already worked with Ryan as producer on an English programme from Wales on BBC 2 called *Poets and Pints*. Geraint himself told me that he felt strongly that Ryan's versatility and talent should not be confined to Wales and, in fact, that he'd been working behind the scenes trying to create opportunities for Ryan in London. In a converstion I had with him, Geraint outlined to me how he had gone about it.

> GSJ: Billy Cotton told me that Ryan was the talent, and that although they felt that they could no longer support the double act, they were prepared to develop Ryan's career. If Ryan had lived, he would have worked in London, because he wanted to show that he was talented enough to swim with the big fish. The possibility of finding a role for Ryan

in a situation comedy on the English network was discussed with Jimmy Gilbert, head of comedy in London. One series had the working title *George and the Dragon*. Obviously, he would have been the dragon.

HG: Were you conspiring with others to bring about the end of the double act so that you could concentrate on Ryan's career?

GSJ: No, there was no conspiracy at the beginning, but things were moving in that direction.

HG: Was Ronnie made aware of the discussions you were having with London?

GSJ: Put it like this. Ronnie did us all a favour, those of us who wanted to concentrate on Ryan's future. From Wales' point of view, the double act was looking tired, and it had lost its spark.

Ryan and Ronnie went their separate ways in May 1974 after Ronnie took his pyschiatrist's advice. The morning after the announcement, Ryan spoke to Alex McKinty from the *South Wales Echo*, and told him how he felt about Ronnie's decision:

I don't want to sound cruel, but I'm relieved I'm on my own. We were both limited as a patter act. Now I'm singing better songs, I'm performing better and I feel happier. I feel I'm able to develop and perform with more freedom.

Not one single word about Ronnie. No mention at all of Ronnie's important contribution to the partnership, as the straight man and the writer of all their comedy material. Ryan had already begun to realise his dreams of being independent. And Ronnie? He was on a painful journey along a rocky road that would take him, in the end, to the bridge over the river Teifi in Cardigan where he ended his life twenty-three years later.

Flavour of the month

Irene, Ryan's wife, was always very supportive of her husband, and he often turned to her for advice. But after the split with Ronnie, Ryan decided that he also needed a personal assistant and a manager. Mike Evans was the young man who fitted the bill – he was manager, personal assistant and chauffeur, all rolled into one. Ryan and Ronnie had met Mike when they were working in the Grand Theatre, Swansea and he was in charge of Radio City at Singleton Hospital. They talked then about their glittering careers, and how everything was going fine, and how they were looking forward to the panto season at the Grand. Now that Ryan and Ronnie had parted company, things were different. Ryan had moved up a gear, and was working even harder than before. Mike soon realised that he was driving someone who was mentally on the move all the time, even when he was relaxing in the back seat of a car on the A470. In conversation, he described to me a typical day in Ryan's life.

Mike would pick Ryan up in the morning from his house in Langland, on the outskirts of Swansea, and drive him two hundred miles to Bangor in north Wales, where Ryan would give an after-dinner speech before being driven across the Menai Bridge to Anglesey. There he would do two cabaret spots, one in Amlwch and then another later on in the Trearddur Bay Hotel. There was no overnight stay. Mike would drive Ryan back to south Wales to be ready for the rehearsal of a light entertainment series at nine o'clock. No wonder he tried to persuade Ryan to work less for more money.

I used to ask him: why don't you halve the workload and double your fee? As his manager, all I could do was just about manage to keep up with him. He lived his life as if he knew it was going to be short.

Mike's remarks reminded me of the words of James Dean, the young American actor who died at the age of twenty-four. 'Dream as if you'll live for ever, live as if you'll die today.' Of course, Ryan worked hard not because he was afraid of dying at a young age, but because he had no other choice. He was hooked on work. It was like a drug coursing through his veins, an integral part of his make-up. Ronnie was an alcoholic. Ryan was a workaholic from the first moment he stepped on the table in the Angel pub in Glanaman as a young lad to sing to the customers for pennies. He never listened, even to his own doctor, when he was told repeatedly that he was working too hard for his own good, and that he ought to take things easy. It would take a bad asthma attack, followed by a heart attack, to slow him down for good.

He died at the age of forty, having achieved so much in such a short space of time, but with so much left undone. A film he appeared in the year before he died was a celebration of Ryan's comic talents on the one hand, and on the other, testimony to the hard work he always put in to every project he was involved in. The film, directed by Richard Lewis, was called *How Green Was My Father*, a satirical reference to the 1941 Hollywood film *How Green Was My Valley*, which was a romanticised view of life in the Welsh Valleys directed by John Ford, who got the feel for the Welsh way of life by shooting the picture in Malibu Canyon, Los Angeles. In his film, every miner sang on the way to and from the pit, every Welsh boxer was better than any other boxer in the world, and every Welsh 'Mam' stood at the top of the table sawing away at a loaf of bread, preferably wearing a shawl, and singing a Welsh hymn at the same time. 'A coal tip of clichés,' according to Richard Lewis. In his film, Harri Webb's script told the story of Jenkin Jenkins the Third, Jr., who has come back to Wales searching for his relatives and his roots. Since everyone in the Valleys, according to Harri, not only looks the same, but is also related, rather than have different actors playing the various parts, why not have Ryan play them all, like Alec Guinness in *Kind Hearts and Coronets*? One review described the film as:

> A virtuoso comic performance, showcasing Ryan's brilliant comic creations ranging from a lusty barmaid to a cheeky schoolboy, via a decrepit reverend, a nasty headmaster, and an out-of-work miner.

There are visual satirical references throughout the film to classic Hollywood cinema as well. When Jenkin Jenkins steps onto the empty platform of Jenkinstown station, we are reminded of a similar scene in *High Noon*. The film ends with Jenkin Jenkins standing alone, in Jerusalem chapel cemetery, with the grey-slated gravestones all around him, and the rain pouring down. 'A tour de force,' according to one newspaper review.

No other actor in Wales at the time could have emulated Ryan's achievement, and he relished the challenge and the hard work. Gaynor Morgan Rees knew better than most how hard Ryan was working, and that it was starting to take its toll on his health. She remembers one occasion in the television studio, when she had to physically support him because he'd had an asthma attack off set. He always carried his asthma pump with him, and a bottle of white medicine for his stomach pains.

When Gaynor asked him sardonically whether he was working

hard because he wanted to be the richest man in the graveyard, his reply was typical of his attitude towards his work: 'You've got to keep doing it while you're the flavour of the month, while they still want you.'

Gaynor played the part of Ryan's daughter in a popular situation comedy series called *Fo a Fe*, about the tensions between a religious, poetry-loving, organ-playing north Walian, Ephraim (the 'fo' of the title), played by Guto Roberts, and Twm Twm (the 'fe'), an argumentative, left-wing, pigeon-loving, band-playing south Walian, played by Ryan. Back in the 1970s, according to popular belief, the Gogs and the Hwntws didn't get on at all, and didn't understand each other because their Welsh accents were so different, coupled with the fact that there was very little traffic between north and south Wales. Indeed, there was a joke making the rounds that only half the audience understood half the programme, depending on whether you were from the north or the south. Twm Twm belonged to the Alf Garnett school of diplomacy, and believed that the north Walians should stay in the north.

Twm Twm: They should build a wall from Aberystwyth to Builth Wells, to stop you Gogs coming down here.
Ephraim: There's no point arguing with you.
Twm Twm: Fify miles of barbed wire, twenty-two yards high. Passports, and visas, and a big sign saying *All Gogs is verboten*!

Gaynor recalls that they recorded the series in Birmingham, and bussed the audience into the studio from various parts of north Wales and local Welsh-language societies.

It's natural for the actor, when he sees an audience, to want to project. But of course, although there was an audience watching us, the one we were performing to was the audience at home, and Ryan had a tendency to forget about the unseen audience and to overact. One evening, we had to finish recording earlier than usual because Ryan had a subsequent engagement in a nightclub. It was strange to see him on set as the argumentative Twm Twm with a muffler round his neck, a flat cap on his head, wearing a coat that was slightly too big for him, and then appearing two hours later in his dinner jacket as the suave, confident cabaret performer with the smooth voice and the slick moves. We all stayed in a hotel in Birmingham, and Ryan was never short of company. Success is an aphrodisiac, and he sparkled in front of an audience wherever he was.

Ronnie put it another way: 'If there were only the two of us in the car, Ryan wouldn't say much. But if there was someone else in the back as well, then that was an audience as far as he was concerned. So, he'd perform. Ruth Madoc, who co-presented *Poets and Pints* with Ryan on BBC2, analysed his charisma differently. 'I thought he was a very sexy man, and I'm sure a lot of women felt the same.'

Ryan Davies meets Sammy Davis, Jr.

Ryan smoked a menthol cigarette as he told me how he was developing his act to appeal to an international audience. His ambition is sharp, and his two-year plan to hit the big time fills him with excitement and zeal.

If proof were needed that Ryan had his eye on the big prize, there it is, in his own words, in an interview with Alex McKinty of the *South Wales Echo*. However, another journalist, Graham Jones, writing in the *Guardian* after seeing Ryan performing without Ronnie by his side, expressed his doubts as to Ryan's ability to compete on the international stage.

> He was always the best of the Ryan and Ronnie partnership, and it was felt by some that he should have gone it alone long ago. He is a tremendously versatile comedian – he can sing well, dance, tell a good story, do impressions, and has shown considerable talents as a straight actor. Yet, I wonder. I miss Ronnie. Ryan seems to me to need a partner, a butt for his humour. In spite of his versatility, his appeal as a comic is limited in range, and I doubt if it can be exported.

Graham Jones' comments are interesting when taken in the context of a one-man show in English which Ryan recorded in the Double Diamond Club in Caerphilly in October 1974. The show had a particularly American feel to it, although it was being broadcast on St David's Day the following year. To the sound of Benny Litchfield's Big Band playing the introduction to the opening number, Ryan comes in and hits the vocal: 'I wanna be happy, but I won't be happy, till I make you happy too.' Close your eyes, and you hear the voice of one of Ryan's heroes, Sammy Davis, Jr. Open your eyes, and you see Sammy Davis, Jr. The only difference is the colour of his skin. Like his American counterpart, Ryan is small, has a nose like Mr Punch, he moves gracefully, is light on his feet, he sings effortlessly. In the Ryan and Ronnie days, the emphasis in the act was on comedy with a song at the end. The emphasis now is on the music and the songs, and in fact, he seems to be happier when he's singing than when he's telling jokes, which he does with a Valleys accent rather than as Ryan Davies. Does this imply that he's happier when he's hiding behind a funny character? Later in the show, after singing 'You are my Sunshine' in the style of Elvis Presley, without naming him, he introduces the star of the show, who also comes from America, and who arrives on stage carrying a candelabra with the red candles already lit.

'Liberace' sits behind the piano in a large, white wig, a larger bow-tie and an even larger set of false teeth. When he smiles, we notice that the teeth are, in fact, coloured like the white and black notes of the piano. With a broad, fake smile, he announces that he is going to play the waltz of the Blue Danube, which he does, with all the style and panache of Liberace himself, ending the show, after a quick change, with yet another American classic, 'My Kind of Town (Chicago is)'. It's surprising in a way that he doesn't respond to the rapturous applause of the audience by singing 'New York, New York', expressing his desire to be 'King of the hill, top of the heap'. Interviewed yet again after the show in the Double Diamond Club, Ryan says that he could see himself singing in the best venues in the future, and not in village halls:

'I could do the clubs for the next fifteen years, but unless they are the Double Diamond, or dare I say it, the Las Vegases of this world, I wouldn't want do that.'

You may remember that a bust of Ryan stands in the BBC in Llandaff, bearing the quote from him: 'Laughter is the same in both languages.' Perhaps we could add, 'but it pays better in English ... and it certainly does in America.'

*   *   *

In the meantime, Ronnie had moved to his wife's home in north Wales to try and escape his past, and all that had gone before. He was hoping for a new start, and a quiet life. He'd tasted success, and that success had left a bitter taste in his mouth that not even a large vodka could obliterate. Years of travelling, and the constant pressure of maintaining standards, had left their toll. Unlike Ryan, Ronnie didn't possess an unlimited store of energy. When the partnership ended, he found himself in a dark place, suffering from depression, according to Dafydd Huws, the psychiatrist he went to see during that final week in Caerphilly. In Ronnie's words,

> It wasn't a break-up, but a breakdown. There was no petrol in the tank. All the strength had been sucked out of my body. I also felt sidelined towards the end. During production meetings about the *Ryan and Ronnie* series, any suggestions I made were ignored, while Ryan was always listened to.

If this sounds like self-pity on Ronnie's part, it was. In the early years of the partnership, he was quite happy for Ryan to have all the plaudits. But as the years went by, he began to crave some of the adulation which he felt the audiences always reserved for Ryan.

Before the split, Ronnie and his then wife, Einir, had started discussing the possibility of moving to north Wales and running a pub. His father, Iori, had kept the Black Horse pub in Carmarthen, and one called the Polyn before that. Ronnie knew the Cerrigydrudion area very well, especially the golf courses, from the time he was dating Einir. So when they heard that the tenants of the White Lion were retiring, they contacted the brewery, and within a few weeks, the whole family – Einir, Ronnie, Arwel and Bethan – had left Cardiff to begin a new life in the north.

Having a famous television personality running a village pub was a big attraction, and when word got around that Ronnie was going to build an extension, albeit without the brewery's knowledge or consent, it soon became a very popular venue for singers and comedians on a Sunday night. He borrowed money from friends and got a substantial loan from the bank. He even persuaded Ken Dodd himself to do the official opening, which he gladly did for £1,000. Ronnie was very generous with his welcome, or in this case, with the brewery's welcome. The actor Dafydd Hywel remembers calling at the White Lion with a rugby club group from Cardiff. Ronnie was drinking with locals when they arrived, and stayed drinking with them while the rugby boys went behind the bar and helped themselves.

One of the most popular singing duos in Wales at the time were brothers Emyr and Elwyn. Emyr was the singer, Elwyn played guitar and Dilwyn played the piano. Ronnie had invited them to the Lion, and having heard them rehearsing, called them over and told them point-blank that Emyr was the one with the talent, and that Dilwyn and Elwyn should concentrate on supporting him.

'But,' Ronnie told Emyr, 'you'll have to change your name. What are you going to call yourself?' Emyr thought for a moment. 'I listened to the radio a lot when I was a boy, and I loved a character called Gari Tryfan.' 'That's it, then,' said Ronnie. 'You're Gari Williams from now on.' And the rest, as they say …

Sometimes, the friends that Ronnie used to perform with would call to see him when they were in the area: Alun Williams, Bryn Williams, Janet Thomas and Ryan as well. Einir remembers one Sunday night in particular, when she and Ryan went upstairs and came down fifteen minutes later, having dressed Ryan as Phyllis the barmaid, complete with mascara and lipstick. Ryan took his place behind the bar, talking in character to the customers, with Ronnie interrupting with the occasional line – just like the old days. Although there were rumours that Ryan and Ronnie were thinking of getting back together, it was never going to happen. Ronnie enjoyed stepping back into showbiz, but only for one night. No more than that. In the Lion, he had a ready-made audience who enjoyed hearing about the days of the white Jaguars when they used to tour Wales, and the season in Blackpool when he and Ryan rubbed shoulders with the stars. He still did some acting on the radio, and would leave Einir to look after the Lion while he went down to the BBC's radio studios. But there was another reason for his visit. Although he had told Einir that his relationship with Lavinia, whom he had met in the good old days on the pier in Blackpool, was over, he was still seeing her in Cardiff. And there were bad old days to come. Einir returned to the White Lion one afternoon while Ronnie was in Cardiff, only to be welcomed by the official receiver. Ronnie was bankrupt. He owed the bank, the brewery, and the Inland Revenue a total of £28,000, which is £280,000 in today's money. He had to sell the family house in Cardiff to pay his tax bill, and Einir moved into a local council house with the children, Bethan and Arwel – but without Ronnie.

The beginning of the end

By the mid-1970s, after Ryan and Ronnie had gone their separate ways, Ryan was as busy as ever, but the offers of work that Ronnie received were few and far between. There was an erroneous belief, even among directors and producers, that although Ryan could be a successful solo performer, there was no future for Ronnie without Ryan. In 1977, leaving his broken marriage behind him, Ronnie moved to Bangor to work as a marketing officer for Cwmni Theatr Cymru. Ironically, he was now responsible for filling those venues in Wales which he and Ryan would have filled to overflowing three years earlier.

In his spare time he started writing again, and the result was a pantomime based on the story of Prince Madog discovering America, with Ronnie as the director. Of course, Ronnie knew how to make an audience laugh after his experience with Ryan during panto season in the Grand Theatre in Swansea, and he'd created a part for himself as well, as the doctor on the journey, with Gari Williams, Ronnie's discovery, playing the part of the North American Indian chief. According to one of the actors, Cefin Roberts, Ronnie wasn't happy in his role as director, and having only a minor part.

> He was an actor. He wasn't happy being in the background. That's why he used to make his entrance as the doctor from the bar, through the auditorium onto the stage. It was a message to the audience: 'Do you know who I am? Don't you remember me with Ryan? Well, I'm on my own now – and I'm still working.

Ronnie was very happy to be working with Gari again. He enjoyed creating visual jokes as he had done for the television shows with Ryan. The memory of those years he spent with Ryan pained him like an open wound, and Gari was the healing balm. On tour, Ronnie was the unofficially elected entertainments manager, and since he knew all the pubs in Wales from his early touring days, and every landlord remembered him and Ryan and those wild late nights, he was made more than welcome wherever he went. He was the heart and soul of every social occasion, but it was a troubled soul for all that. There was a dark side to his character which surfaced without warning, sometimes with dire consequences for those around him, as his first wife Einir could testify.

> Ronnie was living in the Castle Hotel. He was a very heavy drinker by this time. I remember one weekend when the children, Arwel and Bethan, had gone over to spend a few days with their father. Ronnie had been drinking, and he left them in the hotel by themselves and drove the sixty miles to my house. He parked his car where no-one would see it, broke into the house and waited for me to come home. I came back later in the evening. He was waiting for me at the top of the stairs as I went up. He rushed down, pushed me back. I managed to protect myself and push him out, and he drove, in his drunken state, back to Bangor.

Under the influence of alcohol, Ronnie often behaved irresponsibly, and he gave the impression at times that the rules of acceptable behaviour didn't apply to him. And as the heavy drinking increased, so did his mental health problems. While working for the theatre company in Bangor, he decided to organise a raffle, with the money supposedly going to the company. He sat on the prom in Llandudno selling tickets, while some pretty girls approached the visitors and tried to persuade them to take part in the raffle. The prize was a Mini. But no-one ever saw the car. Hundreds of tickets were sold. No-one ever saw the money. How much money was made, and where did it all go? How did Ronnie, who was a bankrupt by this time, manage to get a licence to hold a raffle in the first place? Ronnie left Bangor with all these questions unanswered, and went back to Cardiff, where he got a job as a taxi driver for Castle Cabs.

*   *   *

The camera follows a taxi down Park Place in the direction of Queen Street and Cardiff city centre. It pulls up by the New Theatre. Ronnie steps out and looks up at the poster. The camera cuts to a close-up: *The Sunshine Boys*, a comedy by Neil Simon starring Bill Owen (*Last of the Summer Wine*) and Ryan Davies. The camera cuts back to an over-the-shoulder slow-motion shot of Ronnie, tracking with him as he goes into the theatre, through the auditorium and onto the stage. We look at the audience from Ronnie's viewpoint. They recognise him, and are up on their feet, screaming and shouting their welcome. Bill Owen is slightly confused by the audience's reaction to Ronnie's arrival, and leaves the stage. Ronnie turns and walks towards Ryan, and they embrace as they did in the Double Diamond Club in Caerphilly, when they realised that their partnership was coming to an end. Now they're reunited, and they carry on where they left off, performing together once more.

Ryan did act in that play in the New Theatre, Cardiff, in 1976 with Bill Owen, but the above scene never took place, in real life or on film. A family member of Ronnie's did tell me that, on a visit to north Wales, he and Ryan had discussed the possibility of re-establishing the double act. Knowing them both as I did, I doubt that very much. Ryan was happy now that he was on his own, and although the thought might have crossed Ronnie's mind in one of his darker moments, he was in no fit state to even consider a reunion. Ironically, *The Sunshine Boys* tells the true story of two American comedians, Willie Clarke and Al Lewis, considered in their day to be the greatest vaudeville act in America. Lewis decided to leave the act, and Clarke never forgave him. However, eleven years later, they come back together to make a television programme about the history of comedy.

By the mid-1970s, Ryan had increased his English output and was anxious to concentrate on acting and writing in the future. 'Versatile' was one word often used to describe him, but Jack Williams, who succeeded Merêd as head of light entertainment at the BBC in Cardiff, suggested that Ryan's versatility could be a disadvantage to him, and that he would be better off concentrating either on his singing, his acting or his comedy. Like Ronnie, Jack Williams thought that Ryan's strength lay in his acting ability. Before the play opened, Ryan spoke to the *Western Mail* about his part: 'Perhaps, if I make a success of acting an elderly American Jew, I would like Welsh people to say, "Well at least he can get out of that Welsh thing."' But judging by what the critics said, *The Sunshine Boys* wasn't the success Ryan had hoped it would be, and there was no escape from that 'Welsh thing', because, ladies and gentlemen, boys and girls, it was panto time at the Grand Theatre, Swansea! Ryan was playing Jack in *Jack and the Beanstalk*, and his daughter, Bethan, remembers helping him backstage with the props, while his son Arwyn sat in the theatre with the other children, watching his father thrilling a packed audience. But going into pantomime without a break after the play in the New Theatre wasn't a good idea, and Ryan was taken ill, complaining of stomach and chest pains. When the director went to visit him, he was shocked at how ill he looked. He stayed away for ten days, and although his doctor had told him to rest even longer, he insisted on going back to the Grand. His work schedule had increased, and his asthma had got worse. In addition to the pantomime every night, he was doing cabaret and charity events while at the same time preparing for another comedy series. His big problem was that he couldn't say no to anyone. He even said 'No' when he should have said 'Yes' to his doctor, Brian Cronin, when he told Ryan that he ought to go to hospital for a thorough examination. Ryan refused, saying that he'd arranged a family holiday in America. But first, there was a panto to finish, and another series of *Poets and Pints* to be recorded, and an appearance on the *Wyn Calvin Show* to be made.

According to the song, 'There is nothing like a dame', and there wasn't a dame in any pantomime in Britain at the time who was anything like Wyn Calvin. And yet, he was the first to acknowledge that Ryan's performance over the years in the Grand had been exceptional, but that Ryan and Ronnie's *Good Old Days* show in Blackpool hadn't been a success. He felt that their Welsh humour was too parochial. Ryan, according to Wyn, was prepared to adapt the material in order to broaden his horizons and please the punters, but Ronnie was against any change. As a result, instead of being allowed to carry on until the end of the season in November, their contract was terminated. They were paid off in August, and Wyn himself stepped in when they left Blackpool.

Wyn was known as the Clown Prince of Wales, and he was a frequent visitor to the USA, lecturing on the history of comedy to various Welsh societies. In conversation with Ryan after the show, Wyn felt that he was very interested in visiting America as well, to find out how difficult it would be for someone like himself, who had made it here, to 'make it there', and then 'make it anywhere'. A month later, Ryan and the family were on their way to America to stay with Brian Jones, Ryan's best man at his wedding. Both families travelled through Pennsylvania, Ohio and down to Washington before returning to Buffalo, where Brian lived. They then planned to fly back to Wales – and work. Only two days after arriving back in Wales, Ryan would be starting intensive rehearsals of three one-act plays by Molière, playing the lead in each. Two writers in London were already starting work on the series Geraint Stanley Jones referred to in a previous chapter, *George and the Dragon*, and in the spare time he didn't have, Ryan was hoping to write an opera on a biblical theme. Even God rested on the seventh day, but not Ryan! Was a fortnight's holiday enough of a break to prepare him physically and mentally for the pressures ahead? We will never know, because on his final night in America, he was taken ill with a very bad attack of asthma, and died in hospital of a heart attack.

The change in the weather during their stay in America was partly to blame. It was snowing when they arrived, and then turned warm by the end of the second week, causing an increase in the humidity level, which in turn exacerbated Ryan's asthma. He was rushed to hospital, and after a thorough examination, the family were told that his lung had collapsed. According to Ryan's doctor, who had an opportunity to inspect the body on its return to Wales, had the hospital tried to reinflate the lung after its collapse, small marks would have been visible on the skin, proving that the procedure had been attempted. According to Brian Cronin, there were no visible puncture marks, and he therefore demanded an investigation into what had happened, maintaining that, had Ryan been in Swansea's Singleton Hospital at the time, he might not have died. But in Irene's words, 'An investigation wouldn't have brought Ryan back, so what was the point?' Having suffered two heart attacks, Ryan died in the West Cenotaph Hospital, at 5.30 a.m. on 22 April 1977. Back in Wales, a brief headline in the *Western Mail* told the story: 'Comedian Ryan dies in America'. His body was flown from John F. Kennedy Airport to Heathrow, and Mike Evans was there to meet the family. Ironically, while on holiday, Ryan had sent Mike a postcard which read: 'Get ready, the act goes American from now on.' Perhaps he had his tongue firmly in his cheek, but it shows that performing in America was still on his mind, still a dream, but a dream that sadly would never be fulfilled.

Ronnie was on tour with the Welsh Theatre Company in Colwyn Bay when he heard of Ryan's death. A close friend, Siôn Eirian, remembers walking into the Prince of Wales Theatre and seeing Ronnie sitting alone in the dark auditorium, 'staring in front of him as if he'd seen an apparition.' Was he remembering, perhaps, the number of times he and Ryan had crossed the Severn Bridge, returning from a gig late at night, and how Ryan would always say, 'There we are, Ron, back safely. If I die now, at least I'll die in Wales'?

Alun Williams, another friend and colleague, was presenting an outside broadcast in the village of Groeslon in north Wales, when the local postmistress interrupted the recording with a knock on the door of the village hall. According to Alun, 'The audience stood up, and bowed their heads, as the whole of Wales did in the forthcoming days.' Ryan's death had touched the hearts of the whole nation. And yet, the funeral was to be a private affair. Only the family would attend. No exceptions. Ryan, of all people, was a public figure, and the public would have appreciated the opportunity to pay their respects and express their grief at losing someone who had brought so much happiness into their lives. But the decision had been made, the funeral arrangements completed, and a notice in the *Western Mail* from Irene on behalf of the family left no-one in any doubt: 'The service will be private. No flowers except from the family. No letters. Thank you.'

In Irene's own words, 'We had to accept that Ryan belonged to everyone while he was alive. But I was angry when people tried to claim him when he died. After that, he didn't belong to them. He belonged to us.' As far as Irene was concerned, it wasn't Ryan the comedian, actor and singer who was being buried next to his father in Old Bethel cemetery in Garnant, but Ryan, her husband and the father of her children. Irene told me that she lived with the pain of losing Ryan for years afterwards. 'After he died, I existed, but I wasn't alive. Eight years later, when Bethan received her degree, was the first time I had managed a smile since Ryan's death.'

A few days after his funeral, a remembrance service to celebrate his life was held, appropriately enough, in the Grand Theatre, Swansea, where Owen Edwards, controller of BBC Wales at the time, referred to Ryan as the 'ordinary Welshman with extraordinary talents, who knew his audience, from Glanconwy to Glanaman, through both languages. He always aimed for perfection and, wherever he went, this conjuror of happiness left a trail of laughter in his wake.'

Poets from all over Wales, including some who had won the Crown or the Chair at the Eisteddfod, paid their glowing tributes, but we'll leave the last word to someone who never got the last word when they were working together on stage – his partner, Ronnie.

You couldn't know Ryan without loving and admiring him. There was never anybody like him, and there won't be anyone like him again. He gave and gave of himself all the time. That's how he was. I used to tell him all the time that he was working too hard. I remember one concert where the audience just kept on clapping and shouting for more. In the end, Ryan shouted back at them, 'What do you want? Blood?' In the end, that's what they got.

The many faces of Ryan Davies. With Olwen Rees, Ronnie and the author, recording a pantomime for children's television

Twm Twm, the Welsh-speaking Alf Garnett

He came, he saw, he conquered

This town ain't big enough for the both of us

Ryan and Ronnie in 1967

Ready or not, here we come!

Left to right:
Ryan, Bryn Williams, Mari Griffith, Ronnie

Where *did* you get those frilly shirts, boys?

Fooling around with the
famous Mexican bandit
Johnny Tudor on the left

The surreal world of
children's programmes

Ryan, Olwen Rees
and their puppets,
entertaining the children
of Wales

On the *Ryan and Ronnie* show with Margaret Williams, Bryn Williams and Myfanwy Talog

Bryn Williams, Ryan, Alun Williams and Ronnie –
the Barbershop Quartet

Singer Heather Jones joins
Ronnie and Napoleon Davies

Veteran actor Stewart Jones kicking
out Ronnie, Ryan, Bryn Williams, Mari
Griffith and Alun Williams from his
B&B in Criccieth

On location in Portmeirion, Mexico!

Filming the Wild West in wild west Wales

Myfanwy Talog, Ronnie, Bryn Williams and Ryan – women of the WI

Ryan and Ronnie with some of
their fellow performers

Listen here, gw'boi

You sign, Ron, I'll just smoke
this big fat cigar

Signing the real contract. Second from left: Meredydd Evans, who created the double act

'This is it then, Ron – the big time.'

Ry, are you sure that knot's
not too tight?

About to record a live programme, Ryan sees a mouse

The final song

You know what, Ron? Sometimes you get up my nose!

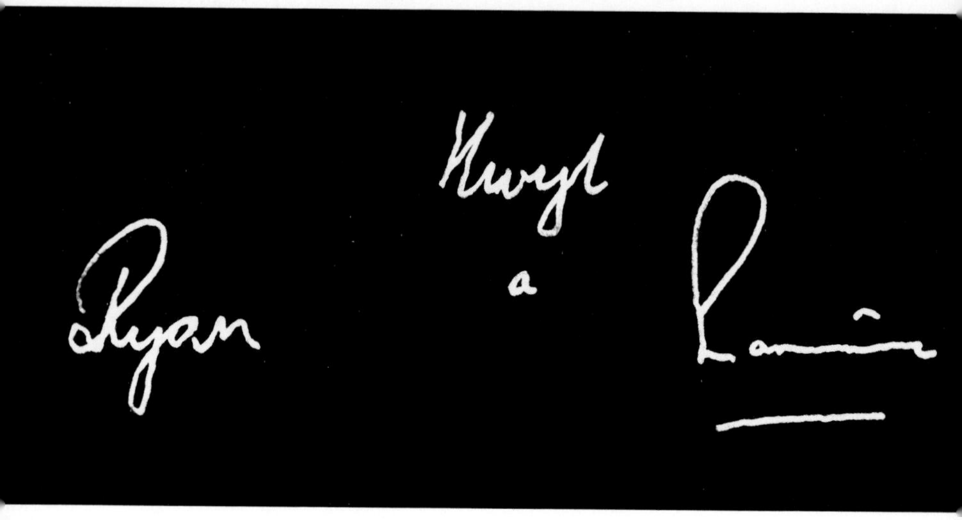
Ryan
a

Ronnie's ghosts

Ronnie's time as a taxi driver was short-lived, and he was soon back in the BBC as a continuity announcer and newsreader, doing exactly the same job he had been doing before he and Ryan formed the comedy duo almost fifteen years previously. He went back not from choice, but from necessity. He needed the money. His first love was performing and acting, but Ronnie was always seen as Ryan's straight man. No Ryan, no Ronnie. No Ryan, no work. Siôn Eirian, a close friend of Ronnie's and a writer for the BBC, maintains that Ronnie went back to work for the BBC because he felt that to be known as a 'BBC man' gave him a certain status in society. Alun Williams, who was one of the best all-round broadcasters in both languages during the 1960s and 1970s, always signed his autograph: 'Alun Williams, BBC'.

Ronnie always looked smart in a clean shirt and tie, a blazer and grey trousers with a sharp crease in them, hair neatly brushed. Witty in conversation, his humour had a dark side to it. He always spoke about Ryan with admiration, but when the vodka was flowing, he'd give vent to his innermost feelings and his resentment about not getting the recognition and acclaim he deserved for writing every *Ryan and Ronnie* series for BBC Wales.

Ryan was always in the spotlight and Ronnie felt that he was always sidelined. I was fortunate enough to know both of them, and to work with them on stage and in the studio. I remember a conversation I had with Ronnie a few months after Ryan had died, when he talked about his relationship with the public.

When Ry was alive, they'd always ask me: 'What's it like to work with him? It must be great.' And when Ryan died, they'd ask me: 'What was it like to work with him? It must have been great.' They never talked to me about me, only about Ry. They never asked me how I was.

He should have realised that the foundations of a house are never seen either, but without them the building would collapse. The public never knew how important Ronnie's role as a writer was. He was the driving force behind the comedy duo. Ryan's light shone brightly like the star that he was, while Ronnie stayed in the shadows, and over the years those dark shadows became all-consuming.

At this time, the BBC Club in Cardiff was a paradise for the heavy drinker. Ronnie felt at home there, so much so that after a few weeks he was made an honorary member of a very exclusive society – the Ceerdiff Langwij Society. Its aim was to keep the language of Cardiff alive, and to protect its unique accent. Frank Hennessy, the Cardiff-born folk singer of Irish extraction, was its first president, and Ronnie was elected as the society's translator. His job was to translate anything Frank Hennessy said in the meeting from Ceerdiff English to recognisable English. As Frank put it, in a way that only Frank could, 'Our Ron, bruv, talks proper, like.' The society had its own archbishop, who could walk just as 'tidy' as any Archdruid, carrying his shepherd's crook adorned with a golden cockle, and he was always followed by the Keeper of the Laverbread. Female members of the Society were expected to wear red or green underwear, which was checked by the official Knicker-checker, who had a wing mirror strapped to a long cane to make sure that they conformed with the society's rules (remember that this was a long time ago).

It was all a bit of satirical fun aimed at the Welsh Language Society, the Gorsedd of Bards at the Eisteddfod, and the Welsh-language establishment in general. At the end of every meeting, all the members would stand to attention while the Ceerdiff Langwij Society's anthem, was sung with fervour:

I'm Cardiff born, I'm Cardiff bred,
And when I dies, I'll be Cardiff dead.
They'll build a little home in Splott
In memory of me.

Apart from occasional shifts as an announcer and newsreader, work was very scarce for Ronnie. He dubbed a few cartoons, made a few guest appearances on children's programmes, and that was it. All the while, he depended on the kindness of friends to put a roof over his head. He stayed with Ryan's close friend, Rhydderch Jones, for a while, who in turn asked John Pierce Jones, an actor Ronnie had worked with, if he could take Ronnie for a night or two. According to John, Ronnie arrived with his cases and his car full of clothes, far more than was necessary for the agreed 'night or two'. Although he was penniless, somehow or other, with his friendly banter and more blarney than a pub full of Irishmen, he persuaded a local car firm to let him hire one of their vehicles. Two months later, the firm took the car back from him. Ronnie hadn't made any payments.

According to John, he would do things on the spur of the moment, and he recalls a time when Ronnie met an American woman and her daughter in a pub in Dinas Mawddwy, which in itself sounds like the beginning of a very unlikely tale. They got talking, and they told Ronnie they were travelling around Wales, but didn't have any idea where they were going. Ronnie saw his opportunity, and offered his services – paid, of course – as a chauffeur. Eventually the holiday ended, mother and daughter went back to America, and, shortly afterwards, Ronnie received an invitation to go and see them. He worked every hour of the day and night, recalls John, trying to scrape together enough money to pay for a one-way ticket. Ronnie's idea was to earn enough money while he was there to buy a ticket for the return journey. A friend of Ronnie's from his schooldays was living in Las Vegas at the time. Ronnie called him and said that he had come to America to try his luck. His luck didn't last long, and he was soon on a flight home, arriving in Heathrow without a penny in his pocket. He rang John, who came to the airport to pick him up and found him in a dreadful state. In retrospect, this was the beginning of Ronnie's inexorable slide down the slippery slope towards complete dependency on alcohol.

When Ronnie was running the White Lion in north Wales, unbeknown to his wife, Einir, he'd found a flat for Lavinia, his girfriend from the Blackpool days, in Westgate Street in Cardiff, and they spent time together there when Ronnie went down to the capital to work. One weekend, they had an unexpected visitor. When Ronnie opened the door, his mother May was standing in the doorway, waving her handbag in a threatening manner. She attacked Ronnie and handbagged him out of the flat. Lavinia herself told me that story in the bar of the pub she now runs in Cardiff with her girlfriend. Her life has changed in more ways than one since 1979, the year she and Ronnie were married, and the year Ronnie had another one of his eureka moments, which happened pretty frequently, according to Lavinia. This time, his idea was to work the clubs of south Wales with an act called Ronnie and Co. He formed a company with Lavinia and other artists, and his son Arwel was persuaded to go down to Cardiff to live with his father and Lavinia to work on the show as a sound and lighting man. Ronnie and Co. was an attempt to recreate the good old Ryan and Ronnie days, when they filled every hall and club they performed in. But those days were long gone, although Ronnie could never accept that. One evening, he made the mistake of venturing on stage by himself. He never came back for the second half, having been paid off during the interval. Ronnie and Co. was yet another failure, which put a lot of strain on Ronnie's relationship with Lavinia:

> He could be violent. He lost his temper very easily because he was on medication for depression when we got married. His nerves were bad and he drank a lot, and he was lacking in confidence. He used to sit and listen to Barry Manilow records, over and over.

One evening, what started as a row became a fight. Ronnie hit Lavinia, and she walked out of the flat, and out of his life, ending his second marriage. By the beginning of the 1980s, Ronnie was an alcoholic. In his own words, he needed a couple of pints in the morning 'to achieve normality', and of course his alcoholic state affected his relationship with his fellow actors. Sharon Morgan remembers how difficult it was to act with him:

> He loved doing the warm-up before the recording because it reminded him of the shows with Ryan. Acting with Ronnie was a different matter, because if you didn't get it right the first time, he'd panic at the thought of having to do the scene again. I remember once, I closed the door and the knob came off in my hand. Rather than stop, I hid the knob as best as I could, and dropped it when I had the chance. At least we didn't have to repeat the scene.

Whilst working on comedy series *Tomos a Titw* in Caernarfon, apart from the three-pint corpse-reviver every morning, Ronnie went to the local pub every afternoon to top up his alcohol levels. He had an interesting arrangement with the landlord of the Black Boy, where he stayed. A large vodka would be placed outside his bedroom every night, not as a nightcap for when he came in, but instead of breakfast when he got up. By this time, he was rarely available for filming in the afternoons, and yet directors and producers were still prepared to offer him small parts on the strength of the fact that the three-hour window in the morning was long enough for Ronnie to be able to give an acceptable performance.

At the beginning of the 1980s, he went back to his roots in the Gwendraeth valley, and was given a job as the manager of the Miner's Welfare in Tumble, where he was also responsible for booking acts to entertain the members on a Saturday night. One ex-miner told me, 'He was ideal for the job. He knew them all from the Ryan and Ronnie days. But there was a small problem with the money, so he had to go.' This suggests that Ronnie was as successful booking acts for the Welfare as he was at organising a raffle for the Welsh Theatre Company. He had a 'problem with the money' then as well, and he had to go – again.

Back to the valley

When Ronnie went back to Carmarthenshire at the beginning of the 1980s, he lived on a caravan site in Cross Hands, down the road from Cefneithin, where he was born, but he spent most of his time on the road, either going to Cardiff to dub cartoons for children's programmes or touring Wales with various theatre companies. Ronnie was the voice of Cracahyll, a nasty old man in a black cloak with a high-pitched, witch-like voice in *The Smurfs* cartoons. Pat Griffiths, the producer, thought he was an excellent actor, and a versatile voice- over arist, in spite of his drink problem, which meant that he was only sober enough to work in the mornings.

> I accepted the situation because I knew that in that short space of time, I would get the performance I wanted, and he always managed to infuse the character with the colorful colloquialisms of the Gwendraeth valley.

1982 was not a good year for Ronnie. He was caught speeding with three times the legal limit of alcohol in his bloodstream, and was banned from driving for two years. During that time, he also lost both his parents, who had been very supportive of Ronnie – too supportive, some would say, and too prepared to help him out of the many financial holes he dug for himself. His sister, Rhoda, tried to persuade her parents not to be so willing to give him money all the time, but rather to urge him to seek help for his alchoholism instead of ignoring the problem. When I talked to people in the community who knew Ronnie and the family, I was told more than once that May, Ronnie's mother, had commited suicide. But the facts on her death certificate contradict that unfounded rumour:

> May Williams, widow of retired coal miner William Iorwerth Williams, 8 Y Fron, Cefneithin, died of Generalised Atheroma and Cerebral Thrombosis. Certified by Huw D. Walters, Coroner for Carmarthenshire District, after a post-mortem.

Had she commited suicide, the coroner would have held an inquest.

Made in Wales was the next theatre company to offer Ronnie a part, that of Jacob Enstrand in their production of Ibsen's play *Ghosts*. According to the producer, Huw Thomas, Ronnie arrived for the first read-through on time, but completely drunk. Why were directors and producers prepared to offer him work when they knew in advance that he was an alcoholic, and could be a liability? The reply was the same, without exception. 'Although you had to be patient with Ronnie, in the end your patience was rewarded, and he always gave you the performance you were looking for.' In the Ibsen play, he gave a commendable performance. The late Huw Ceredig, a close friend and fellow actor during the 1980s, talked to me about Ronnie's dependency on alcohol:

> He couldn't go on stage without the alcohol. He needed it to steady his nerves, and after six or seven pints, he always gave a solid performance. He was very happy to be an actor and not have to live in Ryan's shadow. Ryan was a performer. Ronnie was the actor.

Ronnie was very fortunate that so many of his friends and colleagues were prepared to help him, when it seemed that he was doing very little, if anything, to help himself. One such friend was Siôn Eirian, who wrote a very popular television police show called *Bowen a'i Bartner*. Through Siôn, Ronnie got the part of a shady landlord down in Cardiff Docks. There was an indirect link between the two men, dating back to Ronnie's early days in Cefneithin, when Ronnie was fifteen years old and Jennie Eirian, Siôn's mother, was the Plaid Cymru candidate in the 1955 general election. Ronnie went from door to door distributing election leaflets and persuading people to vote Plaid. When Jenny Eirian died in 1982, Ronnie decided to go up to north Wales to her funeral. Siôn recalls:

> He called in numerous pubs on the way, and although he eventually reached north Wales, he never made it to my mother's funeral. He saw the mourners on their way to the chapel through the window of the pub he was in at the time, and there was something very sad about that.

By the end of the second series of *Bowen a'i Bartner*, Ronnie was arriving consistently late to rehearsals, without knowing his lines and obviously drunk, so the character, and therefore Ronnie, were axed. But Siôn refused to give up on his friend. Since he was also writing for *Pobol y Cwm*, he managed to get Ronnie a commission to write two episodes. Two weeks later, he was still waiting for those episodes to arrive. Eventually, they did – two pages of illegible, unusable notes. But rather than refuse Ronnie's pathetic attempt at scriptwriting, Siôn wrote the two episodes himself and gave Ronnie a credit as joint author, which meant he received half the fee, although he hadn't written a single word.

T. James Jones, minister, poet, author and former archdruid, was the next to help Ronnie, by giving him a part in his play *Pan Rwyga'r Llen* ('The curtain torn'), set in a mental hospital, where Wil Albert, played by Ronnie, is one of the patients, and spends the whole play in bed. Unfortunately for his fellow actors, he used to spend the first act in the nearest pub, since he didn't appear until the second. One night in the dark, behind the curtains, he slipped into bed, ready for the opening of the second act when he made his first appearance, sitting up in bed. On this particular night, he didn't sit up. He couldn't. He was lying in the bed fast asleep. They managed to wake him, and carried on as if nothing had happened. And of course, nothing had happened. As one of the actors told me: 'Acting with Ronnie was a nightmare. He couldn't be relied on to say the lines in the order they'd been written by the author.' And yet he was very fond of reminding people that, unlike them, he'd received two years training in the Royal College of Music and Drama, Cardiff, and was therefore a 'classically trained actor'. In order to prepare for his part, Ronnie had gone to a mental hospital in Carmarthen with the director to observe the patients. After a few hours, the director noticed that Ronnie had disappeared, and went to look for him. He found him sitting on the floor crying, as he remembered the treatment he had received in previous years in the same hospital.

In 1984, acting took a break from Ronnie, and so he tried for, and got, the job of running a very old country house called Tyglyn Aeron, in west Wales. The brewery were obviously unaware that he'd been declared a bankrupt after his unsuccessful attempt to run the White Lion eight years previously. The locals in Tyglyn Aeron, like the locals in the White Lion, were very happy to have Ryan Davies' ex-partner behind the bar, or perhaps at the bar would be more correct, keeping everyone happy with entertainment from popular groups such as the Tremeloes, a group Ryan and Ronnie had met in the Blackpool days. It was whilst managing Tyglyn that Ronnie met Lyn, who later became his third wife. She admitted that when she met Ronnie, she did realise that he had a drinking problem, but didn't recognise that he was an alcoholic. Lyn herself suffers from multiple sclerosis, and perhaps they felt that they'd be able to look after each other, and comfort one another when things got harder, which they certainly would. They were married in the registry office in Cardigan, and one of the guests, actress Sue Roderick, remembers asking Ronnie if he had the ring on him. He didn't. There was no ring. He'd forgotten to buy one. So Sue dragged him to the nearest shop, where he bought a gold plastic one. The shop was Woolworths. Things shouldn't have been able to get any worse, but they did.

Waiting for Godot
and the final days on stage

Chris Monger, the film director from Gwaelod-y-garth, who directed Hugh Grant in the film *The Englishman Who Went Up a Hill But Came Down a Mountain*, directed Ronnie in a long-forgotten film called *Mae'n Talu Weithie* ('It pays sometimes'). Ronnie's first reaction when he read the script was: 'It's about me!' And it could have been. Although it wasn't based on Ronnie's life, it struck a chord in many ways. The main character in the film is a taxi driver who decides to pocket some of his fares in order to spice up his mundane existence. With the police in hot pursuit, he flees to Ireland, where he meets a mother and daughter on a bus to Connemara, who take him to a nightclub (reminiscent of Ronnie's days as a guide to the American mother and daughter tourists). Eventually, he realises the error of his ways and returns to Wales, where he admits everything to the police. His boss speaks in his defence, and so he escapes a prison sentence (which subsequently happened in the 1990s after a court case in Cardigan). Chris Monger takes up the story:

> The film is based on the story of a taxi driver from Ponty. Ronnie begged me for the part. He needed the work, certainly. I changed the lead character's name to Iori [his father's name] for him. He was a delight to work with. Curiously, for someone who had such a body of work, he was almost in awe of us. I didn't understand it at the time, and I still don't.

He was drinking heavily, although it was hard to tell how much. He arrived early in the morning with a pint of beer, and it stayed with him, always being magically topped up. I still don't know who did it. Perhaps it was his wife, who was always close at hand. Despite his consumption, he remained stone-cold sober, never missed a cue or a mark – a consummate professional. But the moment we wrapped for the day, he'd all but sprint to the bar, down a vodka, and a different Ronnie suddenly appeared: maudlin, angry, pathetic, self-pitying, lascivious, silly and funny ... Can I count the Ronnies who appeared? No, but I didn't like them, and had to work hard to avoid him after he hit the vodka. Beer all day? No problem. One vodka, and all hell would break loose. Every night, a fall-down drunk, but he seemed to have no hangover the next day.

Ronnie's erratic behaviour had become his way of life. More work of a varied nature came his way during the late 1980s. He appeared in a television play based on a short story by Islwyn Williams, and in an adaptation into Welsh of a French play called *Pathelin*, set in sixteenth-century France. A gentleman calls three doctors to cure his wife, who has been struck dumb. The three arrive, wearing Eastern clothes which would not have looked out of place in a production of *Aladdin* at the Grand. Eventually, they manage to cure the lady's dumbness by inventing a machine which looks like a discarded contraption from *Charlie and the Chocolate Factory*. I can assure you that the above description is far funnier than the play itself, and it's frustrating that the BBC archives house many plays of such low quality, while good-quality material from this period, including early series of *Ryan and Ronnie*, has been destroyed.

In 1987, Ronnie was touring once again with a production of another T. James Jones play, *Nadolig fel Hynny* ('So that was Christmas'), and Emyr Wyn, a well-known singer and actor currently starring in *Pobol y Cwm*, has vivid recollections of Ronnie's behaviour on one leg of the tour:

> We left after Ronnie had already drunk his statutory two pints of beer for breakfast. We met up with the other cast members for lunch at the Coops in Aberystwyth, then called by the Wynnstay Hotel in Machynlleth later on. Three pints later, it was on to Harlech, where Ronnie ordered a large plateful of sandwiches and another pint before disappearing into the theatre at six, carrying a six-pack of Carlsberg Special Brew.

Every day began and ended with alcohol, and he was making frequent visits to hospital after mixing pills and alcohol too often. Even when Eryl, a friend of Ronnie's from his school days, who had moved to America and was a recovering alcoholic, called to see him, Ronnie still refused to admit that he had a problem.

Meanwhile, back on stage, in his opening scene, Ronnie's character was trying to decorate a Christmas tree and, in spite of all the beer, like the 'brew', his performance was 'special' too, according to Emyr: 'One of the funniest performances I've seen on the stage of any theatre in Wales.' Every time he tried to decorate the tree with the lights, they fused. Every time they fused, Ronnie became increasingly frustrated as he tried to impress on the tree that he was the boss. The audience were in stitches as Ronnie followed his comedic instincts and went 'off script', creating new dialogue, like he used to in pantomime with Ryan, to bring him back to the original story. They had faith in one another's ability to improvise without warning, and Ronnie knew how to play with the audience, like an angler tempting the fish to take the bait. By the end of the 1980s, he was living increasingly in the past, and would arrange Ryan and Ronnie evenings in his local, the Red Lion in Cardigan, where he talked about his time as Ryan's partner and showed videos from his private collection of the shows. Ryan's son, Arwyn, sometimes visited Ronnie for a weekend, and Ronnie loved to show him how talented his father was. According to Arwyn, it was like a masterclass in comedy acting, with Ronnie stopping the machine every time he wanted Arwyn to notice Ryan's sense of timing, or the way a sideways glance could speak volumes. As someone said of actor Huw Griffith, 'He could say more in a wink than others could in a week.'

Arwyn showed very early on that he had inherited his father's talent for songwriting, singing and acting, and the following headline appeared in the *South Wales Evening Post* in 1988: 'Ryan's son is a chip off the old block'. It's a reference to the fact that Ronnie had been invited by Irene to perform an old *Ryan and Ronnie* sketch with Arwyn on the stage of the Grand Theatre in Swansea for a fundraising evening. The evening had the grandiose title 'Night of a Hundred Stars', and for one night only, Ronnie was a star once again.

He was beginning to enjoy working on stage more than in television, partly because nobody was offering him any television work, and in 1988 he landed the role of Pozzo in an experimental adaptation of Samuel Beckett's famous play *Waiting for Godot*. The production was to be a challenge for the audience as well as the actors. The part of Lucky would be played by Judith Humphreys, and she felt that she was indeed lucky to be in a production with Ronnie:

I remember feeling very excited at the prospect of acting with a renowned actor like Ronnie Williams. He was so supportive to a young actress in her twenties. He was very gentle, and although he had a certain confident style, at the same time he was very self-effacing, and there was a certain humility about him. I'm really glad I had the opportunity to get to know him and work with him.

The director, Rhys Powys, decided to stage the production inside a large metal frame representing a cage in a zoo, and the actors visited Bristol Zoo as part of their preparation for the production, to observe the animals and their movements. Then, onstage, inside the cage, they climbed around the metal framework like energetic monkeys. Meanwhile, Ronnie and Judith were waiting ... and waiting ... and waiting ... for Godot. Beckett gave strict instructions in the original production of his play as to how he wanted each character portrayed. He saw Ronnie's character, Pozzo, as 'hypomanic, and the only way to play him is mad'.

The rehearsals for *Godot* were held in Alexandra Hall, Aberystwyth, and each session began with some movement work. Not for Ronnie. 'Men from Cefneithin don't wear tights,' he had said when he was in college, and he stuck to that. He refused to overstretch himself physically either, preferring to sit quietly in the corner of the rehearsal room reading a newspaper, like an elder statesman. But, according to Rhys Powys, he was very happy to experiment with different ideas, some of which were very challenging, others very silly. The cast were given a task one evening to rewrite one of Beckett's scenes in the play, mixing some of their own ideas with those of the playwright. By the following morning, Ronnie presented Rhys with his newly written scene and an explanation:

It has taken me twenty-five years of living in Cardiff to realise that people back home in Cefneithin repeat everything three times before moving on.

Dai and Wil are chatting. Dai is explaining to Wil how a lorry accident happened.

Dai: Yesterday morning, mun ... in the lorry ... down Nant-y-caws hill ... patch of ice ... into the field.

Wil: Jiw, jiw.

Dai: In the lorry ... yesterday morning ... down Nant-y-caws ... patch of ice ... right into this field.

Wil: Go on with you.

Dai: I'm telling you ... Nant-y-caws hill ... yesterday morning ... a patch of bloody ice, good boy ... lorry ... through the hedge ... into the field.

Ronnie would argue that Beckett's dialogue in *Godot* was no more absurd than Wil and Dai's chat in Cross Hands about the lorry accident on Nant-y-caws hill.

Something pretty bizarre, bordering on the absurd, happened one evening when they were performing the play in Llandysul. There was a power cut. The theatre was in darkness, but the actors carried on, and some members of the audience probably thought that being able to hear the actors without seeing them was another of Beckett's absurdist ideas. But Ronnie soon dispelled that theory by shouting from the darkness: 'There we are. A typical Rhys Powys production. I could be on the stage of the London Palladium tonight, but no, I'm in the dark in Llandsysul.' Ronnie walked to the front of the stage and started talking lightheartedly about young people and the modern theatre in Wales, in order to give Brian Sandsbury time to rescue the situation by somehow lighting the set once again. He had an idea. Our hero went outside and drove the large lorry which carried the set around Wales right up to one of the tall windows of the hall, which was then opened, and the lights were shone onto the stage.

Commenting on Ronnie's performance in the play, Iolo Williams, the theatre critic of the Welsh newspaper *Y Cymro*, said: 'Ronnie's performance as the anarchic Pozzo, with his peasant humour and masterly timing, is exactly what we have come to expect of him.'

Beckett would have applauded the critic and the performance, although it could be argued that Ronnie wasn't acting the part. He was living it.

The Dead Stop

Although Ronnie's portrayal of Pozzo in *Waiting for Godot* was very well received, it was to be his last stage performance. He never acted in the theatre again, and his television roles were insignificant at best. Endaf Emlyn, who knew Ronnie from the early days of television in Wales, echoes the sentiments of some producers at the time when he says that they were prepared to employ him because he could still turn in a good performance, but also, possibly, out of sympathy for his fragile state. Throughout this difficult period, when the bouts of depression were far more regular than the offers of work, his wife Lyn was very supportive, even when he made a very unwise decision to manage yet another pub, this time in Llandysilio. The Narberth Arms was known locally as the Dead Stop, because friends and relatives who had been to a service at the crematorium down the road in Narberth always stopped there for a drink on the way home.

Since Ronnie wasn't interviewed by the brewery, we can assume that the licence was in his wife's name. Indeed, he would have had to have put in an Oscar-winning performance to have succeeded in persuading the brewery that allowing an alcoholic who suffered from bouts of depression to run a pub was a good idea. Lyn did all the work, as usual, while Ronnie propped up the bar and kept his customers satisfied by buying drinks for everyone, and showing his collection of old *Ryan and Ronnie* tapes yet again after stop tap. His health deteriorated. He went for long periods without alcohol before starting the heavy drinking once again, and the binge drinking was a sure sign, if any were needed, that he was an alcoholic. On one occasion, he drank so much that he collapsed on the floor in a fit and had to be rushed to hospital.

When he returned to the Narberth Arms, he received a visit from Dafydd Rowlands and Dilwyn Jones, who had established an independent television company called Teledu Daffodil. They were friends of Ronnie's, and they offered him a substantial role in a new comedy series, *Licyris Olsorts*. It was about a group of old characters in the Tawe valley, spending their old age and their pensions, burying their friends and talking about their exploits. Its gentle humour and sharp observations were reminiscent of *Last of the Summer Wine*, but it was very much of the area, and was based on real people that eminent author Dafydd Rowlands had known when his family lived in Pontardawe.

Ronnie was the youngest member of the bunch, but he looked older than all of them. Siw Hughes, who played the part of Deborah, Ronnie's sister, recalls:

> It was sad for me to remember Ryan and Ronnie in their fabulous, wine-coloured velvet suits, and then to see Ronnie's physical deterioration before my own eyes. To be honest, he couldn't be bothered to discuss the scenes before we shot them. He was tired, and he just wanted to do it – finish it, and that was it. Unfortunately, all the drinking had made him very bitter and twisted, so that if he had to repeat a scene nine, ten, and sometimes even eleven times because he couldn't get his words out, or because he'd forgotten his lines, he would blame everybody except himself.

While he was appearing in *Licyris Olsorts*, Ronnie was offered a small part in a film called *Dafydd*, which starred a very young

Richard Harrington, in his first film appearance, as Ronnie's son. In his only scene in the film, father and son look at a panoramic view of the south Wales coalfield together for the last time. The young man has decided to leave home for a more exciting life in Amsterdam – a new life, which will involve him in a gay relationship and a rape. Twenty-five years ago, it was a film that pushed the boundaries, and plenty of people questioned whether it should be shown on television at all. It's true to say that this was the first film in the Welsh language to discuss homosexuality in any depth, and it certainly sparked a heated debate between people of polarised opinions on the matter. But if you cast your mind back to an earlier chapter, you will remember that, thirty years previously, a company called Dyffryn Films made a film about the issues surrounding homosexuality and its illegal status, set in Cardiff. The film was, of course, produced and directed by Ronnie.

Ronnie worked for the last time in 1996. He got the small part of Mr Mort in the Swansea-set and immensely popular film *Twin Town*. When asked why he wanted Ronnie to play the part, director Kevin Allen's answer was brutally honest: 'I wanted an old Welsh icon.' Ronnie was certainly old by then, but he was only fifty-seven years of age. In the final scene of the film, the Pontarddulais Male Choir are gathered on Mumbles Pier with Ronnie conducting them. To the strains of 'Myfanwy', coincidentally one of Ryan's favourite songs, and one of the most beautiful love songs ever written, the camera cranes up for a high shot of the pier and the lights of Swansea dancing like fireflies in the dark beyond. The camera is still moving away from the scene as we hear the choir sing the final words of the song, which take on a new significance in terms of Ronnie's professional career, which comes to an end with this final shot:

A rho dy law, Myfanwy dirion,
I ddim ond dweud y gair 'ffarwél'.

Give me your hand, my sweet Myfanwy,
but one last time to say 'farewell'.

*　　　*　　　*

He used to carry a small flask of vodka with him, and
sometimes, when he was having a coffee, he'd pour a
drop into the cup. Lunchtime, he'd sit at the bar, reading
a newspaper … He liked a bit of peace and quiet at that
time of day. Towards the end of the afternoon, he'd go off
to the golf club and carry on drinking.

That's how Maisie, the owner of the Red Lion in Cardigan,
remembers Ronnie. She also remembers the 'Ryan and Ronnie
evenings', when Ron would reminisce about the old days, and show
a video or two of them in their heyday. The urge to perform was
still there – in fact, when the Eisteddfod came to Carmarthenshire
in 1996, Ronnie had booked a function room at the Golden Grove
Hotel for three nights, where he intended to make some money by
talking about his past in broadcasting, showing a few *Ryan and
Ronnie* programmes and answering questions from the audience.
The audiences never came. It was a complete flop. Indeed, the last
night was cancelled, and to add insult to injury, an evening of
singing and poetry, arranged at the last minute, filled the empty
function room to overflowng.

By the end of 1996, Ronnie's physical and mental health were
a cause for concern. According to one friend, he had asked him
what would happen if he stuck his finger in an electrical socket

or placed his head in an oven. Ronnie, it must be said, was well known for his dark humour. Nevertheless, he did confess that he had contemplated 'going to the bridge' and throwing himself into the river after a court case where he was accused of stealing £1,789 of raffle money, which he had purported to raise for the Multiple Sclerosis Society. His wife Lyn was a sufferer, of course, and the money was supposed to go towards buying a machine to treat patients locally rather than having them travel to Swansea. The main prize was a Fiat Bravo car bought from a local garage in St Dogmaels and, according to the owner, Ronnie had somehow or other managed to get a loan of £15,000 to buy the car. It became clear during the court case, however, that Ronnie owed money to the bank and others, and was living on benefits of £66 a week. Tickets were sold on the streets of Cardigan, and hundreds were bought at the Royal Welsh Show in Builth Wells before the raffle was cancelled. This was the third time that Ronnie had arranged an illegal raffle. When asked in court what had happened to the money, Ronnie's reply was that it gone on expenses: phone calls, hotels, and payments to the bank for the loan he had. Even his own son, Arwel, had warned him to look after the money: 'I told him to take it straight to the bank. But he didn't. He kept the money, wrote a cheque, and the cheque bounced.'

The defence called Huw Edwards, a psychiatrist, as an expert witness. He maintained that Ronnie's mental faculties had deteriorated to such an extent that he had become hypomanic, like Pozzo, the character he had played in *Waiting for Godot* several years previously. Ronnie could no longer differentiate between right and wrong. During the case, he changed his plea to guilty to the illegal lottery charges, and was given a year's suspended jail sentence. He was found not guilty of stealing the money and the judge's final words came as a warning to him:

You musn't become involved with anything like this again. You paid no attention at all to the requirements of the Lotteries Act, and let down very badly not only those who trusted you, but the charities involved. I accept it was your intention that the charities would have benefitted [from the funds raised].

After leaving court, Ronnie was whisked away in a car belonging to the HTV current affairs programme *Y Byd ar Bedwar*. He had agreed to talk to them before the court case, seeing it as an opportunity to tell his side of the story, and to justify his actions to those in Cardigan and beyond, who were adamant that he had got away lightly, and should have gone to prison. The programme contains a lengthy interview with Ronnie conducted by Betsan Powys, who is now editor of BBC Radio Cymru. He is sitting on a hillside looking out over Cardigan town and the bay. He hasn't shaved, and he looks scruffy and tired, with a wild, frightened look in his eyes. His slurring speech makes it difficult to understand what he's saying at times. The person talking is an alcoholic, with mental health problems, who has tried to commit suicide on a number of occasions. It's important to ask, when listening to his words: are they sincere and honest? Are those tears genuine, or are they the tears of an experienced actor, trained to create the illusion of genuine emotion? At times, he is angry and bitter and shouts at the camera. Full of self-pity, he believes that he's been forgotten by friends and shunned by colleagues who really didn't want to employ him, and actors who didn't want to work with him after Ryan's death. On the contrary, this book has shown that, throughout the 1980s and 1990s, theatre and television producers had employed him, supportive writers had commissioned scripts from him, directors had worked patiently with him, spending valuable time they didn't really have to get that performance they believed he could deliver. In fact, it could be argued that he'd had more support than he really deserved, and that the truth was that Ronnie was unwilling, or unable, to help himself.

From the end to the beginning

Following the court case, Ronnie suffered a heart attack and spent two months in Glangwili Hospital. On another occasion, he returned there after taking an overdose of pills, with the intention of committing suicide.

On the Saturday before Christmas Day 1997, Maisie remembers him in the Red Lion, by himself:

> I was very busy, so I didn't talk to him. Looking back, I regret it. If I had gone over and had a chat, things might have turned out differently. That was the last time I saw him.

Arwel, Ronnie's son, was worried about his state of mind after talking to him on the phone, and came down from north Wales to see him, and to persuade Ronnie to spend Christmas with him. But Ronnie said he wanted to stay where he was. As he left, Arwel told his father that he loved him. He would never see him again

*   *   *

The body was discovered by Peter Bodenham from St. Dogmaels, and pulled out of the river at a place which was difficult to reach, between Ferry Inn and Teifi, near Graig Pool. Ronnie's body had been in the river for seven days, and the watch on his wrist read 2.08 a.m. on 22 December. Arwel still has his father's watch. Neither the time nor the date have been changed.

When the body was discovered, no-one realised at the time

that it was Ronnie, thinking that it was the body of a French sailor from a fishing boat which had been lost at sea since Christmas Day.

The police went into Ronnie's flat to try and find evidence of his movements before his suicide. They found two television sets on their sides on the floor. On the sofa, there were numerous empty bottles of diazepam, Nytol and paracetamol. On the table, two brown envelopes contained a message each for Angharad, Ronnie's stepdaughter and her mother, Lyn. The message to Angharad thanked her for looking after him: 'Gone to God for peace. Thank you for your help. Ronnie xxx'. The wording on Lyn's envelope was formal and unfeeling: Mrs. M. L.Williams, of no address, or anybody's. The message inside read: 'Although the way you behaved towards me during the last two years was awful, I loved you 'til the end. Sleep peacefully, if you can.'

His body was taken to the local hospital, and at 4 p.m., it was confirmed that the body was that of Ronnie Williams, Feidr Fair. According to the post-mortem, he was suffering from congestive cardiomyopathy, and cirrhosis of the liver as a result of excessive drinking, and a dependency on benzodiazepine.

According to the coroner, Michael Howells, Ronnie had killed himself, and he added:

> Ronnie's career never recovered from the untimely death
> of Ryan, and the sad history we have heard shows what
> deterioration can happen when a close relationship in a
> top act is destroyed by the death of one of them.

In a tribute to him, Dafydd Rowlands, author of *Licyris Olsorts*, who knew Ronnie well, had this to say about the days when Ryan and Ronnie were at the top of their game:

They were wild, heady days, when Ryan and Ronnie enjoyed the excitement of driving those white Jaguars in the fast lane, and the thrills were sweet and the success justified. But life is not all about the peaks. There are troughs as well, and some are deeper than the sea and darker than the night. Ronnie knew about those as well.

Although Ronnie's funeral, on 26 January 1998, was a cold and rainy affair, hundreds came to Parc Gwyn Crematorium in Narberth to pay their last respects. The previous week, the *Western Mail* had noted his passing in a three-word headline bordering on the derisory: 'Comic's body found'. Those words would have angered Ronnie. 'I'm a character actor, not a comedian,' he said, more than once, after his partner's death. 'Ryan was the comic.' He'd read the news, interviewed and presented on television and radio, but he liked to think of himself above all as a talented actor. He once said that Ryan could do everything, but that he was better than Ryan at three things: ping-pong, billiards and acting. And he meant it.

The simple funeral service was presided over by the Reverend Elfed Lewis, who had been a friend of Ronnie's since their primary school days in their home village of Cefneithin. Elfed lived in the manse in School Road and Ronnie lived further up in Maesteg, past the house of a frail boy who, in spite of his mother's attempts to stop him playing rugby, played for his country, and became one of the most respected coaches in the game. He would hide his shorts and rugby boots under the hedge at the bottom of the garden, so that when his friends called, young Carwyn James was ready. Years later, sitting on that grassy verge overlooking Cardigan, and baring his soul to the camera a few months before he took his life, Ronnie spoke about Carwyn, and another of

Cefneithin's famous sons who became a rugby legend: 'Wales can be a cruel little country. They were cruel to Carwyn James, they were cruel to Barry John, and they've been cruel to me.' The truth is that family, friends and colleagues had supported Ronnie throughout his life, especially after Ryan's death. Only one person steadfastly refused to help Ronnie, and that was Ronnie himself.

The congregation could hardly have expected the Reverend T. James Jones to open his tribute to Ronnie with the words 'Bloody Christmas'. In fact, they were the opening words of his play *Pan Rwyga'r Llen*, in which Ronnie had appeared ten years earlier, and they gave full vent to his feelings about losing Ronnie during the festive season. 'Ronnie knew,' said his friend, 'that there is only a fine line between laughter and tears, not only on the television screen, but in real life as well.'

The congregation sang two hymns, and the final curtain slowly closed around the coffin. The mourners left, with Angharad, Ronnie's stepdaughter, supporting Lyn in her frail state. Angharad was the one who had looked after Ronnie in his final months, trying to persuade him to eat more instead of killing himself slowly with the constant flow of alcohol and pills. But she knew in her heart of hearts that her fight to keep Ronnie alive was one she could not win. As she admitted herself, 'He had gone down and down, and there was no way back up.'

*   *   *

To most people, Ronnie was Ryan's straight man, and no more than that. Ronnie was Ernie Wise, Ryan was Eric Morecambe, end of story. But Ronnie was a producer, a director, an actor, an impersonator, a scriptwriter, a presenter and a newsreader, in English and Welsh, on radio and television, and he'd had years of experience in broadcasting before establishing the comedy double act with Ryan. So on that cold winter's day in Narberth, we in Wales lost a talented man who, like his talented partner, died too young. However unappreciated Ronnie felt in life, that cannot be denied.

*   *   *

A few weeks after the funeral, the family took Ronnie's ashes back to the Gwendraeth Valley and scattered them on Llyn Llech Owain, the lake where he had played as a young boy.

Acknowledgements

I would like to thank the following people:

Ceri Wyn Jones from Gomer Press, for asking me in the first place, and for saying I could when I thought I couldn't.

Irene, Einir, Lyn and their families, for their help. Without them, this book would not have been possible.

Edith and Gwen in the BBC Archives, for being so generous with their time and expertise.

Luned, my editor, for her guidance, for showing me the way and, at times, showing me the way not to.